Jimmy Rees, aka Jimmy Giggle of ABC's *Giggle and Hoot*, is a household name whose videos became a public service during the pandemic, giving audiences a good laugh when the headlines were anything but amusing. A regular on Australian television and now with his headline comedy show *Meanwhile in Australia* sold out across the country, Jimmy has become a multi-generational favourite and one of the most-watched social media personalities of recent years.

THE GUY WHO DECIDES

AUSTRALIA'S FUNNIEST SOCIAL MEDIA SENSATION

JIMMY REES

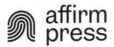

affirm
press

Published by Affirm Press in 2022
Boon Wurrung Country
28 Thistlethwaite Street
South Melbourne VIC 3205
affirmpress.com.au

10 9 8 7 6 5 4 3 2 1

Follow, subscribe, visit, connect:
Instagram: @jimmyrees_
Facebook: jimmyreesofficial
Ticktok: jimmyrees
Twitter: jimmyrees
Youtube: JimmyReesComedy
Website: Jimmyrees.com.au
Management: Red Management
Contact: info@redmgmt.com.au

 A catalogue record for this
book is available from the
National Library of Australia

ISBN: 9781922806437 (paperback)

Cover image by Jimmy Rees
Cover design by Luke Causby, Blue Cork
Typeset in Trade Gothic Text LT and Felt Tip Woman by Post Pre-press Group
Proudly printed in Australia by McPherson's Printing Group

Include one of those quotey things from someone I've barely heard of to impress the readers — TGWD

'To give a satisfactory decision as to the truth it is necessary to be rather an arbitrator than a party to the dispute.'

— Aristotle

CONTENTS

A WORD FROM THE AUTHOR

Hello, sir. I think you're meant to say something here.

> What are you talking about, Jason? Have you been drinking?

Oh no, sir. That's your department.

> Correct! Slurrrrrp.

So, what are you going to say, sir?

> About what, Jason?

The book, sir. Remember? We spoke to those people who said you have a book in you.

> Jason, Jason, Jason. I think I'd know if I had a book in me. Last time they checked, they said there was nothing there but a couple of polyps.

Err, I was talking about you *writing* a book, sir.

> Nobody reads books, Jason.

I don't think that's true, sir.

> Shut up, Jason! I read about it on Facebook.

Well, anyway, a lot of people are very excited about you doing a book, sir.

> I'm the Guy Who Decides, Jason! I'll decide what's exciting. What happened to my drink? Refill!

Of course, sir. There you go, sir. I just thought the prospect of being a bestselling author might—

> Shut up, Jason. I'm thinking. Slurrrrrp. And now that I've thought about it, I might just be interested in this book thing. But only if I get to decide the title.

Um. That should be okay, sir.

> Of course it should. My book is to be called *The Guy Who Decides: The Story of a Genius Who Succeeded in Spite of His Idiot Sidekick, Whatshisname.*

A little harsh, sir.

> All right, all right. Make it … *His Idiot Sidekick, Jason.* You can't ask for more than that.

I wouldn't dare, sir.

> But wait. What sort of book is it exactly? Oooh, is it a romance? Do I get a mysterious love interest? Wait! No. I'm the mysterious love interest. What a saucy minx.

I don't think that's quite it, sir.

> A thriller, then? With me as the suave detective and decider of whodunnit?

Not exactly, sir.

> An exposé, then? A journalistic tour de force with me at the decision-making epicentre, with a steely glint in my eye and a leather jacket over my shoulder. Yeah. Do that.

Sir, I don't think—

> Shhh! I can see it now. I'm going to win a Pewwww-litzer!

Let's not get ahead of ourselves, sir.

> Don't be a Jason, Jason. What would you know about getting ahead of anything?

You're right, sir. Good point, sir.

> So, when does it start?

When does *what* start?

> The book, you idiot!

Oh, right. Let me check. It seems to have already started.

> Already?! But I haven't done my hair! Who's in charge here?! Did we open with one of those impressive quotey things to make me look extra smart?

Probably, sir. You are in charge, sir. Remember?

> Well, don't just stand there blinking at me, Jason. Get typing!

I don't think that's how it works, sir.

> Shut up, Jason! Get on with it!

I think we need words, sir. From you.

> Typical. I have to do everything around here. Are we ready, then? Are we rolling?

It's not a video, sir. It's—

> SHUT UP, JASON! And get out of my shot. Hello, dear readers. As you know, I'm the Guy Who Decides, and I've decided you should read this book. Why? Because it's a masterclass in decision-making. After all, life is a series of decisions and I probably make 2000 of them a day, no problem. But how do I make it look

so easy, you ask? Well, let me show you. What you do is you get a glass just like this one and you fill it with gin, or vodka or anything alcoholic, really ... sluurrrrp.

Ummm ... is that it, sir?

Shut up, Jason! I was pausing for effect. Of course there's more to it than that.

Oh, good. For a second there I thought you'd forgotten that this book isn't *all* yours. There'll be other stuff in here too.

My apologies, dear readers. Jason can be very rude sometimes. SHUT UP, JASON! Now. Where was I? Oh, yes. The trick, dear readers, is to say the first thing that comes into your head. Like, say, two L's!

Sorry, sir. What?

Keep up, Jason! I have decided to spell Lloyd with two L's.

Oh. Okay. So, Llinda should have two L's too? And Llaunceston?

Jason, Jason, Jason. Now you're just being an idiot ... sluurrrrp ... Thankfully, my readers are much smarter than you. Ignore him, dear readers. As I was saying, in the following pages I'll teach you the art of stress-free decision making — my way, naturally. I'm even going to show you what to do when you are faced with a Jason. And let's be honest here, we are all often faced with a Jason. But hey, no biggie. I didn't become the leading decision-maker in the country without having a few tricks up my sleeve to deal with Jasons and other problems. So, sit back, relax, and let me share with you all of my best decision-making secrets. Jason! Get over here! This glass won't fill itself!

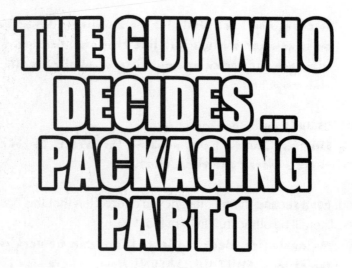

THE GUY WHO DECIDES ... PACKAGING PART 1

Hello, sir. I've got a new list of products here. What should we put strawberries in?

> Put them in a little box that you can see through.

Okay. And blueberries?

> An even smaller box that you can see into.

Oookay. And broccolini?

> Just put a little elastic band around it. *Slurrrrp.*
> A purple elastic band. It must be purple.

Right. Oranges?

> A net.

Potatoes?

> A sack.

Lemons?

> People can get them themselves.

6

Grapes?

> Just a little plastic bag with little handles on it.

Pumpkin?

> Chop it up and wrap it in plastic.

Mushrooms?

> A paper bag!

Okay. Yoghurt?

> Put it in a tub with a little paper lid.

Jam?

> Jaaamm. Put it in a glass jar with a metal lid that goes *pop* when you open it. Haha.

Okay. Vegemite?

> Put that in a glass jar too.

With a metal lid that goes *pop* too?

> No! A *plastic* lid, what are you, stupid!

Oh, right. Okay. Milk?

> A waterproof box with a little triangle at the top.

Um. How will they open it?

> They'll figure it out. Oh. And if it's over a litre, put it in a plastic bottle with a handle and a plastic lid. Yeah. Do that.

Juice?

> That can go in a waterproof box too.

With the little triangle at the top, sir?

> No! What are you, an idiot? How would they get into it? Put a little circle lid there that they can twist off.

And what if it's over a litre? Put it in a plastic bottle with a handle?

> Noooo! People who drink juice don't need a handle. Just make it a bottle with no handle.

Right. Um. Tomato paste?

> Put tomato paste in a yoghurt tub, but with an aluminium lid. Not a paper lid. Haha.

Chips?

> A bag.

Flavoured biscuits?

> A bag. Wait! Put the bag in a box.

Right. Snap-lock bags?

> Well, put them in a box.

Storage boxes?

> Put them in a bag.

DVDs?

> Put them in a plastic box that doesn't break.

CDs?

> Put them in a plastic box that does break.

Sliced white bread?

> Plastic bag.

Gourmet bread?

> Paper bag.

Tomato sauce?

> Put it in a bottle in the shape of a cone.

Soy Sauce?

> Put in a glass bottle with two openings so if you tip it one way it comes out and if you tip it the other way it comes out too. Why not?

Scissors?

> Put them in the hardest plastic you can find. The kind of plastic you'd need scissors to get into. Hehe.

Tuna?

> Put it in a can. With a little ring-pull thing so you don't need a can opener.

Beetroot?

> That can go in a can too.

And add the little ring-pull thing so you can get into it easily?

> NO! You need a can opener to open the beetroot.

Okay. Long-life milk?

> Waterproof box.

With the triangle bit like the milk? Or with the little lid, like the juice?

> Noooo! They have to make a hole themselves.

Of course.

Slurrrrp. Well, look at that. I'm all done.

Oh, but there are more, sir.

Nah, gotta go. Byeeeee!

THE GUY WHO DECIDES ... WEDDINGS

Hello, sir. What if people want to show their commitment to one another?

> That's easy, Jason. Just get one of the two to buy a gift for the other.

Oh, great!

> I'm thinking a small piece of metal to go around one of their fingers, Jason.

That sounds nice.

> And then put a massive diamond in the middle of it. A huge one!

Err, won't that be expensive?

> *Pffffft*. Of course it will be, Jason! So expensive that it creates financial hardship.

Right. That's a great way to start a life together. And what finger does this expensive thing go on?

> The one you can't control. Haha. *Slurrrrrp*.

Right. Put a weight on a finger that you can't control. Seems logical. What about the other half of the couple, sir? Do they get a gift too?

> What are you, an idiot, Jason?! No gift for the other person! Not yet!

Oh, right. What else?

> They're going to have a party, Jason. The bride and groom will go on a diet and go to the gym, so that when the party's over, they'll never look like that ever, ever again.

Oookay. What's the dress code?

> Formal, Jason! Except the bride will wear a white dress that she can't breathe in.

That sounds, err...

> And she'll wear a net over her face.

A net? ... What about the groom?

> I'm not finished with the bride, Jason! The bride will also wear ... a train! A big, long train with lots of carriages. Haha!

A *train*, sir?

> You heard me, Jason! A train!

Right, so I'm guessing she'll be sitting down then.

> Jason, Jason, Jason. No. The bride will walk down a path, in front of everyone. So that if she falls over, it will be very, very embarrassing! Slurrrrp.

12

No pressure, then.

> But *this* is the best part, Jason. A random person will stand up the front trying to crack a few jokes, but no one will laugh because they don't know who this person is. And then the random person will make the bride and the groom enter into a verbal contract, before signing an actual contract.

Right. So—

> I'm not finished, Jason!

Great. *Sigh*. There's more.

> There'll be a moment when the random person asks the audience if anyone else wants to marry the two people up the front. Haha!

Shouldn't that have happened before?

> Don't be a Jason, Jason! Think of the drama. Hehe.

Right. And does the groom get his gift *now*?

> Yes, Jason. For once in your life, you're right. He gets a little ring.

And I'll put a massive diamond in the middle of it as well?

> No, Jason! He gets a pissy little ring!

Okay, sir.

> And the bride gets another ring.

Another one? That doesn't seem fair.

Jason, you're skating on thin ice.

Okay. Um. Go on?

No! I'm bored now. Just make the bride and groom walk back the way they came while everyone throws crap at them. And then they can wander off for five hours to have photos taken, while everyone else gets drunk, and then the bride and groom can do a silly dance, cut a cake and go home. Ha! I'm out of here. Slurrrrp.

Ummm … do they live happily ever after?

Gotta go, Jason!

What are we deciding tomorrow, sir?

Divorce!

THE GUY WHO DECIDES ... AUTOCORRECT PART 1

Excuse me, sir. We need to help some people with a little correction.

> Well they've come to the right place, Jason. What's first? Slurrrrrp.

Okay, first up we have: 'I can't find the *epicen*.' What do you think that might be?

> Epic penis.

Um. You think, sir?

> Yes, Jason! Send it.

Oookay. Sent. Next one: 'OMG. I am getting *marr-dried*.' Hmmm. *Marr-dried*? I think they mean married, sir.

> Murdered, Jason. I am getting murdered.

Um. Do you want to take another look at that, sir?

> Stop messing around, Jason! She's getting murdered!

Okay. It's sent. Now we have *defintly.* Then another *defintly.* And another. Ooh, a *definiately.* And then a *defintly* again. Then basically another 38 *defintlys.* Should we just send them back as *definitelys*?

People can't spell definitely, Jason. Send them all.

All right. Here's one: 'I am in a lot of *paon.*' Pain?

Porn.

You don't think it's *pain*, sir? I am in a lot of *pain*?

No, the person is clearly in a lot of porn. Send it.
Okay.

And this one? 'I will be there at *sox.*'
Do you think they meant—

Sex.

No, I was going to say *six.*

You heard me, Jason. It's sex. It makes perfect sense. I'll be there at sex. Send it!

Okay. It's sent.
Um, sir, we got *epicen* back again. Should I just try *EpiPen*?

Epic penis, Jason. It's epic penis.

Right. Sent. Moving on. Oh, this one seems correct. So does this one.

Wait! What was that last one?

It's good, sir. It doesn't need correcting.

Tell me!

16

Um. All right. It says: 'The guy who decides autocorrect should burn in hell.'
Slurrrp.

Sir? Are you okay? You're not saying anything.
Change hell to hello.

Err, okay, sir. Sent. This next one says: 'Thank goodness for the locksmith. I *ilpcked* myself out.' Do you think it's—
Licked!

Oh, see, I was going to say *locked*. As in, *I locked myself out*.
Jason, Jason, Jason.
I've been deciding
things for a very long
time. Slurrrrrp. It's definitely licked.

I licked myself out. Sure. Send.
Next!

Okay, looks like we have *seriously* spelled wrong 3,675,251 times.
Seriously?

Seriously. Let's see what else we've got. Here we go: 'I've just finished my degree. I can't wait to spend my days *hylpinf* animals.' What do you think, sir? *Helping* animals?
Humping.

Oh, but this person is a vet, sir. They've just finished their degree in veterinary science, so—
It's humping, Jason! Send humping. Humping
animals.

17

Okay. I've sent it. Now, this one's getting a bit urgent, sir. We've got *epicen* back again. I really think it's *EpiPen*, and I think they must be looking for it, and that it's kind of a matter of life and death, sir? I'm just going to send *EpiPen*.

> *Pfffffft. Don't you undermine me, Jason! It's epic penis. Send it.*

Um. All right. I'll send *epic penis* again. As long as you're sure, sir.

> *Defiantly, Jason!*

THE GUY WHO DECIDES ... THE ELECTION CAMPAIGN

Elections, sir.

> Make the guy who runs the country be the guy who sets the date for the election.

Okay, what about the other guy?

> Pfffft. No, Jason! There's a reason he's the opposition.

Okay, so the date is set. Then what?

> Campaigning!

What's that?

> Make the guy who runs the country and the guy who doesn't run the country visit random locations around the country and beg for people's votes, Jason.

Beg?

> Yeah!

Okay, where do they go?

> All over, Jason.

What do they do?

> The most random shit ever.

Seriously?

> Like, wear a hard hat, and some high-vis, and weld their own face. Or maybe bowl a cricket ball at a clown.

A clown? What?

> Yeah, a clown, Jason. Or maybe wash some hair in a hair salon.

Really?

> Kick a football! Even though it looks like they've never touched a football in their life, Jason.

Sigh.

> Or go to a school and have the most awkward conversations ever with school kids.

That doesn't sound—

> Hold a baby, go for a morning swim, have—

Sir—

> ... some beer with some blokes in a pub!

Okay. And what else?

> They get asked questions.

20

Do they answer the questions?

> Pfffft. No, Jason! What are you, stupid?! They just say the same crap over and over and over again, like budget, jobs ...

What?

> Healthcare, schools, deficit ...

Climate change?

> Pfffffffffttttt! No, Jason! What are you, an idiot?!

Sigh. And then what?

> Make the guy who doesn't run the country forget some basic facts that he really should know on day one of the campaign. Haha!

No, sir. That would be embarrassing.

> Yeah, it would.

So, we won't do that?

> We will do exactly that, Jason. Slurrrrrp.

Then can we have everyone say something nice about each other?

> Dig up their pasts, Jason!

Sir, no, that's not what I was thinking at all. I thought—

> And they can call each other idiots, and hopeless, and *losers*.

21

Okay. Wait. How do they win the votes, sir?

> They compete to be the least annoying, Jason.

How many teams are there?

> A red one and a blue one.

Only two?

> Ah, fine. Make heaps more. But only two of them can ever win.

What? How is that fair?

> Shut up, Jason!

Please tell me that's it.

> There's more, Jason.

Like what?

> Infighting.

Sir—

> Backstabbing. Lies.

Lies!?

> Promises.

Oh, well, promises are nice.

> Sorry, Jason. I meant broken promises.

No!

> Scandals.

Sir, this is—

> Then more lies!

Sigh. And how long does this go on for?

> An eternity!

Like, forever?

> No, Jason. It's about six weeks. But make it feel like an eternity.

What, like the weather?

> Yeah, like the weather. Like when it's 25 degrees but feels like 35. Yeah. Like that.

You done?

> Yeah, I'm done. Gotta go!

Phew. I think *I* need a drink.

> Do they answer the questions?

> Pfffft. No, Jason! What are you, stupid?!

AD BREAK: COME TO AUSTRALIA!

JIMMY: You may have heard that Australia's international borders are open – fan-bloody-tastic if you ask me – so we're ready for you to come and enjoy all the things—

RANDOM AUSSIE: That can kill ya!

JIMMY: What? No, no, no. Not that! What the hell, man? Shut up! Sheesh. As I was saying, come and enjoy Australia's golden beaches, with rolling waves and glorious sand, and—

RANDOM AUSSIE: Stingers!

JIMMY: Not stingers! Shhh. Come on, mate ...

RANDOM AUSSIE: What's the problem, mate?

JIMMY: Seriously, mate?

RANDOM AUSSIE: Just being real, mate.

JIMMY: Visit our mountain ranges. The bush. The outback. The—

RANDOM AUSSIE: Brown snakes!

JIMMY: No!

RANDOM AUSSIE: Tiger snakes?

JIMMY: *No!*

RANDOM AUSSIE: Red-bellied black snakes?

JIMMY: No, no, no. Come on, mate! This isn't a video about what can kill you! I'm trying to tell everyone that our borders are open and that they should come and see our beautiful country, so can you please—

SOUTH AFRICA: If you want to come somewhere with animals that can kill you, come to South Africa, A lion will literally rip you in half.

JIMMY: What the hell?

NEW ZEALAND: We have deadly animals too, you know.

SOUTH AFRICA: *Pfft*. As if. I've got one word for you: hippopotamus.

JIMMY: No, shut up.

NZ: The redback spider?

JIMMY: What? Wait! That's ours!

NZ: No, it isn't.

SOUTH AFRICA: In South Africa, a rhino will flatten you.

JIMMY: Well, hang on, we have crocodiles.

NZ: Wild boar.

SOUTH AFRICA: Awww, that's cute, New Zealand.

NZ: Hey, they have a powerful body and they can be very unpredictable in nature, I'll have you know.

JIMMY: The blue-ringed octopus!

SOUTH AFRICA: The black mamba!

NZ: The katipo spider!

JIMMY: Stone fish!

SOUTH AFRICA: Elephant!

NEW ZEALAND: Grey side-gilled sea slug!

JIMMY: What?

SOUTH AFRICA: Pah. Riiiight.

NZ: Very deadly!

JIMMY: Kangaroo.

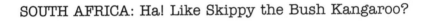

SOUTH AFRICA: Ha! Like Skippy the Bush Kangaroo?

JIMMY: Yeah, well, not that one in particular, but they can be dangerous!

SOUTH AFRICA: No one's scared of Skippy.

JIMMY: Don't be fooled by the pouches, mate. Roos can kill ya.

SOUTH AFRICA: Please, I'm quite fine here. I don't need to go to Australia to get killed by an animal, you know? It's quite sufficient what we have here in South Africa. I could be trampled by a rhino tomorrow if I wanted to be, all right?

JIMMY: Shut up, South Africa. That's not what this video is about. God. Come to Australia, people! The food, the hospitality. It's amazing. Take Melbourne, for instance.

MELBOURNE: Defs come to Melbourne first. We've got the best coffee, and sporting events. Like, the culture here is—

SYDNEY: Shut up, Melbourne. No way. Like people are going to travel all the way to Australia to see the West Gate Bridge. *Pfffft.*

TASMANIA: Didn't that fall down once?

JIMMY: Guys, can we not do this?

QUEENSLAND: If you want some sun, come to Queensland!

SOUTH AFRICA: And hang out with all those cane toads?

RANDOM AUSSIE: Which can also kill ya!

SOUTH AFRICA: Oh, really? A frog?

JIMMY: *Anyway* ... art, music, entertainment, celebrities ... like Chris Hemsworth, Nicole Kidman, any celebrity from New Zealand who we claim as our own.

NZ: Hey!

JIMMY: Shut up, New Zealand! Everyone's welcome!

NOVAK DJOKOVIC: Err ...

SOUTH AFRICA: Well, *that* was awkward.

JIMMY: Shhh! So, get over here, tourists! Come and visit Australia. We're dying to see you! Oh, wait. That came out wrong. There's no dying! I didn't mean ... there's nothing to ... oh, god.

MEANWHILE IN BRIGHTON PART 1

Hello, darling.

                                    Darling.

Darling, did you get your jab?

                    You mean jabs. Yes, darling.

Love it, darling. I just had a fresh Bobo jab.

Oh, you look so smooth, darling. Can you smile, darling?

Absolutely not, darling.

Fantastic, darling.

Darling, I also got another jab.

Do tell.

Darling, I got the Pfizer jab.

The Pfiizer?

Yes, darling. The Pfiiiiiiiiiizer. Have you had your Pfiiiiiiiiiizer? Don't tell me. They gave you the Azeee?!

They gave me the Azeee, darling.

Oh, darling, but you don't look a day over 45.

I know, darling, but apparently it's not how old you look, it's how old you actually are!

Unbelievable, darling. How dare they give you the Azeee.

You won't tell anyone?

Of course not, darling. This stays between us.

Twelve seconds later ...

Girls, girls, come here! I have to tell you something. Kaaaaarin got the Azeee!

She got the Azeee?!
Not the Pfizer!?

No, not the Pfiiiiiizer. Hahahahahhahahahahahhaha hahahhahahahhahahahahahhaha hahahahhahahahaha hhaha!

But wait a mo, darlings. We all got the Azeee too!

We know that! But we'll never tell anyone, will we? Now let's practise, shall we? Pfiiiizer.

Pfiiiiizer.
Pfiiiiiiiiiizer!

MEANWHILE IN BYRON PART 1

Hey, babes.

Hi, babe.

How was yoges, babe?

Yoges was ... ahhh.

Sunrise yoges?

Yah, sunrise yoges.

Nakes?

> Mmm ... well, 98 per cent nakes.

Pics, babe?

> Sure. Jo-Nathan was there with me. You'd better have
> got some good pics, Jo-Nathan!

So what are you up to today, babe?

> I need some new clothes.

White linen?

> Yah, white linen.

You can never have enough white linen. It's so freeing.

> So free.

So free. Oh my god, is that Chris over there?

> Oh my god, really?

Jo-Nathan! You'd better not miss this! We need pics of us
with Chris or it didn't happen! Oh, no, it wasn't Chris. It
was just Liam. But this light, so good, am I right?

> Yaaas.

Jo-Nathan, hello? Are you on your phone?! Oh my god.
You should be getting us in this light! It's gone now,
don't worry. Urgh.

You know, I wouldn't mind a boujee tea.

Off you go, Jo-Nathan! And don't forget — extra fennel and get a pic for Insta before they put the lid on! Love you, babe, thank you!

Oh my god! Have you seen this!?

What is it, babe? Did someone leave a negative comment on your sunrise yoges pic?

No, babe.

Don't tell me you were showing a nip?!

No, babe. We're in lockdown!

What?! No! In Byron?

Ya. In Bryon!

What even *is* lockdown?

We have to stay home for seven days! Oh my god! And did you see this?! There's panic buying already!

No way.

All the shops have sold out of healing crystals in Mullumbimby!

Get out!

I hope they were pre-charged.

Oh, here's Jo-Nathan with our boujee teas. Thanks, babe. Now get a pic of me with my tea, babe.

Get one of me too.

So, does lockdown mean we have to wear a mask?

Yeah, I saw a little market on the corner, selling white linen masks.

Finally. Find them, Jo-Nathan! And follow them on Insta! What? Should you follow them on Facebook as well? Is that a joke, Jo-Nathan? Of course not on Facebook. Just stick to being hot and finding the light for me, okay?

Oh my god!

What is it now, babe?

It says here that some guy from Sydney came to Byron and spread Covid all around and didn't even check in.

No! You mean he didn't take a photo, post it on Insta and tag-harvest? What did you say, Jo-Nathan? The services app? Don't be silly, Jo-Nathan. That's not how influencers check in.

Ooh, babe. The light's good again now.

I'm not in the mood.

I feel you, babe.

I wonder with lockdown if Chris can still go for his morning surf.

Oh, poor thing.

What's that, Jo-Nathan? You can still exercise?

Thank god.

Ya, because we've got sunset boxercise, right, babe?

Oh, but Jo-Nathan says we can't do group.

That's okay, we don't actually boxercise, remember? We just get a pic of us boxing with the sun going down. Don't you know anything, Jo-Nathan?

Oh, but babe. What am I going to do about this weekend? I had a staycation booked.

Ooh, where?

Oh, not far. Still in Byron.

It's so not fair. We bought a $7 million property to escape lockdown. I mean, seriously.

Ya, I can't believe someone brought it here. What a selfish jerk, spoiling our Byron.

HIPPIES: It was ours, you entitled jerks.

Did you just hear something?

No, but I can smell incense.

Babe, that's not incense.

It's just so sad that we're in lockdown. What do we do?

I suppose I could take it as a time to reset, you know? Start my celery juice cleanse.

It will just be so sad to see all those shops closed.

Uh, the shops! And all the warehouses in the Induzzy. So sad.

Oh, no.

What now, babe?

I might have to cook my own dinner!

Don't panic, babe. I'm pretty sure Jo-Nathan will be able to put the celery in the blender. And grate the fennel over the avocado.

Aw, you're the best, Jo-Nathan.

Well, good luck, babes. Jo-Nathan! I need to get a goodbye pic. I don't even care if the light's not right.

See ya, babe.

See ya, babe. I'm off to panic-buy some CBD oil.

THE GUY WHO DECIDES ... PACKAGING PART 2

Hello, sir, we have some new products. Apples?

> Just put a little sticker on them.

Mandarins?

> A sticker.

Kiwifruit?

> A little sticker.

Dragon fruit?

> Sticker.

Limes?

> A sticker!

Pears?

> Just put a sticker on all the fruit, except for bananas. Yeah. Slurrrrrp.

Okay. Still water?

> Put it in a plastic bottle with a little seal on the top. And then put a lid on top of that with a little pop-up thing that you can drink out of easily. And then put a cap on top of that. And wrap it in plastic. Ha!

Don't you think that's a little excessive, sir?

> Don't tell me how to do my job, Jason. What's next?

Eggs.

> Eggs. Hmmm. Make it look like they're on a roller-coaster and they've each got their own seat.

Okay. A roller-coaster. And rice?

> Well, that can go in a plastic bag. And put a little sticker on it, so they can reseal it, but when they reseal it, it doesn't stick.

Oookay. Flour.

> A paper bag that's folded and glued at the top, with a little bit of flour underneath so it goes pfffff when you open it. Hehe.

Mineral water?

> Just a plastic bottle with a lid. But make sure it's shaken up so no matter how slowly they open it, it goes sssssssphhhhhhh all over their hands.

Wine?

>A glass bottle with a screw cap.

Expensive wine?

>Oh, that needs a cork in it.

Lots of wine?

>A silver bag with a tap. And then put the silver bag in a box with a little hole where the tap can poke out. And put some handles on it too, so you can carry around a box of wine. *Slurrrrp.*

Beer?

>A bottle with a twisty lid. And some without a twisty lid. And put some in a can. And they can choose.

Tasty cheese?

>A big rectangular block that's wrapped in plastic.

Parmesan cheese?

>Cut it into a triangle and wrap it in plastic.

Mozzarella?

>Shape it like a snowman. And wrap it in plastic.

Jarlsberg cheese?

>Make it look like a doorstop. And wrap it in plastic.

Camembert?

>Make it into a circle. And wrap it in paper.

Goat's cheese?

>Put the goat's cheese in a jar. And cover it in oil.

Fetta?

Let it swim in its own juices in a bag.

Do you think we should put it in a jar with its own juice?

Nooo! I want it to go everywhere when they open it.

Right. So I've got some long-life items here too, sir. Corn?

A tin.

Fruit salad?

A tin.

Diced tomatoes?

A tin.

Whole peeled tomatoes.

A tin.

Pears?

Tin.

Apples?

Tin.

Chickpeas?

Tin.

Coconut milk?

Tin.

Condensed milk?

A tin!

I think I know where this is going. I'll put the olives in a tin?
Nooo! Put them in a jar. Slurrrrp.

Right. Unsalted peanuts?
Plastic bag.

And salted peanuts in a plastic bag too?
Pfffffft. Nooo! They go in an aluminium bag!

Of course they do. I should have known.
And now you do. Thanks to me. Slurrrrp.

THE GUY WHO DECIDES ... SCHOOL HOLIDAYS

Hello, sir.

> Hello, Jason. Make the kids have a little break from school.

Oh, okay. How long?

> A week. Nah, make it two weeks. *Slurrrrrrp.*

Two weeks? And do their parents have a break from work too?

> No!

Right. Sooo ...

> The kids will be at home for two weeks, Jason.

What will their parents do?

> Make them attempt to do some work from home with all the children running around, Jason.

Really?

> Yeah, really. Or ... they could go on a family holiday.

Well, that sounds nice.

> And make the holidays wildly overpriced, Jason.

What?

> Cram the airports and the holiday parks and all the holiday destinations with people, Jason. Ahaha. Slurrrrp.

Sir, that doesn't sound like a holiday.

> Shut up, Jason!

If people are taking time off work, maybe they've got some holidays saved up, but maybe they're taking unpaid leave to—

> Spend it all on an overpriced holiday, Jason. Yeah.

Well—

> They don't have to go on holiday, Jason.

Well, what do those people do, then?

> Make them attempt to entertain their kids at home, Jason.

Right.

> But make it so that 99 per cent of the time, they fail to entertain them. And even though the kids have 10,000 toys to play with, they go completely wild but are also bored at the same time. And instead of playing with those 10,000 toys, they decide to pull all the cushions off the couch and all the doonas off all the beds and make a fort, which is both inconveniently placed in the kitchen and annoying for the parents.

But, sir, that sound like the—

> The zoo!

What about it?

The parents will want to get out of the house, so they'll plan a trip to the zoo.

Okay, well, the zoo is—

Horrendously busy.

What?

Yeah, Jason.

Sir—

And make the day that everyone decides to get out of the house and go to the zoo 45 degrees and unbearable.

No, sir, no, that's just—

Fine! Make it raining and horrible then.

Sir, no. You can't do that. I'm putting my foot down. No!

Jason, Jason, Jason. You are flying in the face of danger. My face.

Umm.

Make parents get fed up with all the whingeing and whining from their kids. So, they, in turn, winge and whine to their own parents, calling in the grandparents for grandparent duty. And then the kids will behave like complete angels for the grandparents. And then, upon returning to their own parents, the kids will turn into devils again, and the grandparents will wonder what all the whingeing was about.

Right, so what you're saying is—

It's a giant circle of whinge.

Wow. Anything else?

> Holiday programs.

What are they?

> Who cares, Jason. It's babysitting for the kids.

Okay. And do the kids want to go?

> No. What they want to do is stay at home and play Playstation and eat chips all day long in their pyjamas.

But, sir, can we just have *something* positive?

> Shut up, Jason!

Please?

> Fine. Make it so the last weekend of the holidays is moderately pleasant.

Okay!

> People come back from their holidays, and everyone's getting ready for the routine of school.

Great!

> And then, on the first Monday after the holidays ...

Yeah?

> Make it a curriculum day. Hahaha!

What? Nooo, sir.

> You heard me, Jason. Gotta go! Haha!

Honestly, how do you come up with these things?

> I'm empty, Jason!

Of course.

PARENTS R US: IF YOU HAD TO PURCHASE PARENTHOOD

CHASTITY: Hi there and welcome. I'm your consultant, Chastity. So, you're looking at parenthood? Have you purchased any parenthood before?

    HER: Hi, no, we're first-timers.

CHASTITY Ooh, virgins. Well, not *virgins*. But … well, you know what I mean. Let's get started. We have such a wide range here. You guys are going to love it. So, I'm going to set you guys up with a starter pack. That includes paid parental leave for you, madam. And partner leave for you, sir, lucky guy.

    HIM: Err …

CHASTITY: But the pack also includes zero sleep and poo explosions.

    HER: Um, sorry, did you say *zero* sleep?

CHASTITY: Well, by law we have to have the zero sleep in there. Regulations, you know. Blah! Hahaha. But all our starter packs come with the Worry Collection, which includes 11 trips to the hospital – which turn out to be unnecessary, hahaha – slight germaphobia, *and* annoying in-laws. But it's okay because you guys get to choose which in-laws are the annoying ones. So that's fun.

HER: Right.

HIM: Right.

CHASTITY: Ooh, and I know what you're going to ask, and yes, all of those are regulations as well. Now let's talk about kids' food, yay! Okay, so we've got option A, the package called Whatever Will Shut Them Up. That includes your plain cereals, your bread, your plain pasta, the occasional banana, squeezy pouches, a crapload of yoghurt, lollies, chips and, yes, whatever else will shut them up.

HER: Oh, is, um—

CHASTITY: *Orrr*, there's option B, which is your organic purees, your oat milk, your rice milk, *definitely* no nuts, ethically sourced broccoli and cauliflower baby salad, kale smoothies, coconut oil in everything, and carob chocolate for a little treat. Yum! All handmade, of course. By *you*. We also throw in a free Thermomix because you'll just want to fit into the group, you know? If you're in that group, and you don't have a Thermomix, you won't fit in.

HER: Aha. So, which one of these is the most popular?

CHASTITY: Well, first-timers always go for the organic, ethically sourced milk alternative milky, Thermomix-y we're-not-quite-sure-how-they-sustain-it one.

HIM: Oh.

CHASTITY: But people who are purchasing parenthood for a second or third time, well, they pretty much triple-down on option A.

HER: Ummm, so what do you think, darl? I think we go the organic—

HIM: The organic one, yeah.

CHASTITY: Oh, the organic one. Surprise, surprise. Actually, I'd already put that one in. Haha. Now. Let's talk material items. So, again, a few options here. There's Quantity Over Quality, Hand-Me-Down Central or I Can't Fucking Believe They Make Them for Kids. That last one includes your boots from Milan, your cashmere, your fur coats. That's the most expensive one.

HIM: Well, definitely not hand-me-downs.

HER: Ooh, no. We'll go for the most expensive one.

CHASTITY: Interesting choice. I'll put that down. Okay. Let's talk sleeping arrangements. Who is going to remain in the marital bed and which one of you will sleep in the kids' room?

HIM: Oh, well, we'll *both* sleep in the marital bed.

CHASTITY: Unfortunately, sir, that's not an option, no. But there *is* a mattress-on-the-floor add-on. We could go with that. What do you think?

HER: Oh.

HIM: Err.

CHASTITY: You know what? You guys are so lovely. I'm just going to throw in the mattress-on-the-floor add-on. No extra charge. There we go. Now. What's next? Social life. Not applicable.

HER: Really? No social life!?

CHASTITY: Let's see. What else? Overseas trips. We won't need any of those.

HER: Can't go to Milan?

CHASTITY: Ooh, Appearance! This is where it gets fun. For you, madam, would you like extra wrinkles, or the bags under the eyes?

HER: Um ...

CHASTITY: And for you, sir, would you like the grey hair, or the bald?

HIM: Oh. Um. I ...

CHASTITY: I know, it's a tough decision. Take your time.

HIM: Grey? But—

CHASTITY: You know what, guys? You're so nice, so just let me check something. I just have to make a call. Hello? Simon? Yeah, it's Chastity. Can I get an approval on a double double? Yes, I've got this lovely couple here. So lovely, so naive. I know. So can we get the wrinkles and the bags and the bald with the double chin?

HIM: Wait, I said grey hair.

CHASTITY: Oh, sorry, I did say that, didn't I? Simon? Yes, it was the grey hair. Yeah. And then the bald. Thanks so much, Simon. Love you, bye! There we go! I got them both for you both!

HIM: Thanks for that. Um ...

CHASTITY: Just a few more things. Won't be long. Let's see. Oh, kiddy bedtime routine. Did we want the strict routine, or should I just leave that out?

HIM: Well, if I may ask, what's the difference?

CHASTITY: If you go the strict routine, you'll never see anyone at night-time and, if you ever actually make it to a party, you'll always have to leave within the first 20 minutes.

If you go the no-routine option, we will provide you with a dice. So you roll the dice, and that's bedtime! Oh, but I should point out that the dice numbers start at 8, then go 9, 10, 11, 12 and 1. So, who knows?

HER: Oh my ...

CHASTITY: So you'll go with the strict routine, got it. Good luck with that one. Now, we're almost there. I'll just add a snotty nose for nine months of the year. You'll need to get a new car, of course. And here's a list of things you'll need to buy. Did you want me to print that off for you or would you like me to send it as a PDF?

HIM: The PDF, thanks.

CHASTITY: Good choice, because it is 48 pages long. Just a few more things to cross off here. No gym. No golf. No sport on the weekend. I'll add a coffee addiction for you. We did the pooey nappy and lots of spew. Oh, and I have to tell you there *is* a no-returns policy and it *is* 24/7, and if you could just sign here that'd be great. Congratulations!

HER: Um.

HIM: Th-thank you. Ha ...

CHASTITY: Oh, and just before you go, I've added *one* sexy time for you guys. How's that?

HIM: You mean, like, one a week?

CHASTITY: Ah ...

HER: One a month?

CHASTITY: Ahhh ...

HIM: One a *year*!?

CHASTITY: So, anyway, congratulations!

FAMILIES GOING ON HOLIDAY

Because just getting out the door can be so hard ...

MUM: Kids! Get ready! We're leaving any minute now!

DAD: Everything everyone wants in the car, bring it to the front door and I'll put it in!

MUM: Kids! Get off the PlayStation and pack your bags! And don't forget toothbrushes. We always forget toothbrushes!

DAD: Let's go, let's go. We don't want to hit the traffic.

MUM: Now, gotta pack my stuff. It could be cold, so I'll pack a jacket. But it might be really hot, so I'll need all this lighter stuff too. Undies, socks. What if we go out? Hmmm. Yeah, something a bit fancy. And then something else in case we go to the pub one night. Oh, this is cute. And I have to take that. What if we get invited to a wedding at the last minute? Yep, better put this in. Ooh, and I might get some casual teaching while we're there too. Who knows? Some outfits for that. Just in case. Some activewear. You never know. Hey, Siri, what's the weather going to be like? Hmm ... changeable. Right. I'm going to need a lot more of all of that. What'll look good by a campfire?

DAD: Righto. Pack my gear. Jocks. Spare T-shirt. Some pants. Pair of shoes. That'll do me. Hey, where did all these massive suitcases come from? We're only going for three nights?! What, darl? No, no. All good. I'll find a way to fit them in.

MUM: Have you left a key out for my mother?!

DAD: Has anyone taken the bins out?!

MUM: Kids! Have you packed your iPads? And they'd better be charged up! It's the only thing that keeps us sane in the car.

DAD: Come on, kids! Chop-chop. And bikes or scooters? One or the other, okay?!

MUM: Kids! Get off the PlayStation.

DAD: I'm just going to quickly mow the lawn before we go. It's looking a bit long.

MUM: Darl! You need to put the dishwasher on before we go!

DAD: Packing car now! If it's not by the door, it's not going in!

MUM: Just getting some snacks for the car!

DAD: I'm just going to quickly clean the gutters! Hey, darl, who's going to feed the fish?

MUM: Really?! You couldn't have sorted any of that earlier in the week!? My mum's going to feed the fish! Did you check if we could bring the dog?!

DAD: Oh, yeah, sorry! I did check! And we can't!

MUM: Arrrgh! You had one job! Seriously! I have to call Mum.

DAD: Come on! We need to go soon or we'll get all the traffic.

MUM: Mum, hi. Yes, I know you're feeding the fish. Do you mind having the dog as well?

DAD: Right, so I can't fit everything in like this. I'm going to have to reshuffle. Everything out.

MUM: Kids! Get off the PlayStation!

DAD: Do we need to take bedsheets and stuff?!

MUM: Did you get the baby monitor?!

DAD: Ah, can you remind me we need to fill up the gas bottles?! But don't worry, we'll do that when we get petrol!

MUM: Are you actually serious?! You haven't even filled the car up with petrol?! Kids! Off those iPads. Get in the car! Where are your shoes? Come on! Out the door! Dad's almost ready. Where's your pillow? No, it's *not* time for hide and seek! Get out here, now! Have you got your chargers?

DAD: Do we really need the whole box of nappies!? And do we really need the toy Batmobile?

MUM: Are we leaving the dog inside or outside for Mum?! Kids! If you get in the car now, we'll go through Macca's drive-through. In, now! What are you doing? No, you're not having a shower now. I've spent seven years trying to get you in the shower and now's the time you decide to be independent?! Get. In. The car. I'm putting the dog out! And then we're going!

Another hour later.

DAD: Bloody Batmobile. Right. I think we're sorted. Okay?

Twelve seconds later, stuck in traffic.

MUM: You're kidding me. Your iPads are flat?!

DAD: Did anyone lock the front door?

MUM: I'm pretty sure I did. Did you put the bins out?

DAD: Ummm ...

TALKING TO TELEMARKETERS: WHAT'S YOUR STYLE?

THE HAPPY PAYING MORE: Who is this? You're selling what? Oh, sorry, no, I don't need that. Pardon? Yeah, I've already got that, too. Yeah, I'm quite happy paying more, thanks.

THE NUMBER QUESTIONER: How did you get this number? No. I want to know how you got this number. Who gave it to you? A list? What list!? Don't you hang up on me. I need to know—

THE BAD RECEPTION: Sorry ... Look ... can't ... dropping out ... Uh ... nup ... can't hear ...

THE SMART ARSE: Yeah, sure, and can you save me 100 per cent on my power bills? Yeah, if you can save me 100 per cent on my power bills, then you've got my business. Sorry? You can't? Okay, bye!

THE ANGRY ONE: Who!? What!? This is ridiculous! I get a call every single day from you! It's not right! No, no. I'm hanging up now!

 THE SUPER BUSY: Yeah, I'm just really busy at the moment. *So* busy. I've really gotta go. Yeah, call back another time. Tomorrow? Um, no, I'm super busy then as well. Okay? Really, really busy. Bye!

THE SHAMER: Do you actually enjoy this job? What a shocking way to make a living. I mean, honestly. You just annoy people every day, for a living. How many people actually listen to you? Yeah, yeah, whatever. Bye!

 THE GULLIBLE: Okay, yes. Wow. Well, that was quite a chat. Two whole hours! And you've got all my details now? Oh, great. Yeah. Okay. Bye! What a lovely young man. And I'm sure he'll make very good use of my kidney.

THE OVER-YOUR-HEADER: Can I speak to your manager? No, I just want to speak to whoever is in charge there. Yeah, I know you're still talking but I just want to speak to your manager. Just put your manager on!

 THE REVERSER: Hello, you've called, um, Energy Saver Protect. If you'd like to save, err, money on your energy bill then just listen to my spiel that I'm about to rattle off. What's that you say? You're a telemarketer too?! That's weird. Well, does your call centre want to save some money on a great deal? Thought not.

THE IMMEDIATE END: Hello? Ugh. *Click.*

THE SILENT TREATMENT: Hello?
.... *Click.* Oh, they hung up. Thank god.

THE LEAD-ON: Do you know what? I am interested in saving money on my power bills. Yeah! How much can you save me? Wow. You know, I just love listening to you talk. Can you repeat all that for me? Great. Now let me go and find my power bill and credit card details for you. Not at all. So I just have to sign a few forms that you send me? Okay, great. What's my address? Aw, I've forgotten it. No, I really have. Straight out of my head. Aren't I a duffer? Bye!

THE KIDS EXCUSE: Yes, I am the homeowner. But I've got the kids here right now. I've got all the kids. Every single one of them. And they haven't eaten. And they're starting to throw furniture. What's that? Can't hear you! Gotta go!

THE GUY WHO DECIDES ... FORMULA ONE

Fast cars, Jason.

Okay, sir.

The fastest in the world, around a track, Jason.

Wow.

Make them look fast too, Jason.

Okay. Sounds cool. So, there's a lot of action and overtaking and—

No.

Come on, sir. Let's put it in from the start. Action, overtaking and—

Pffft. Shut up, Jason! The cars are fragile! And they need a bit of a cuddle.

A cuddle, sir?

Yes, Jason.

But shouldn't we make them resilient?

Jason, Jason, Jason. I make the decisions around here. The cars will have a safety pod that is basically indestructible.

Ah, that's better.

> And that's where the driver sits. But the rest of the car could be destroyed if you sneeze a bit too close to it.

What? Really? Well, what about the drivers?

> Make them small and skinny.

Um.

> But with a massive neck.

A massive neck?

> Yeah, for all the g-forces, Jason.

Right. And how many cars are there?

> Ten.

Okay.

> Times two.

So, 20?

> Make it ten pairs of cars. Yeah, do that.

Okay. So, 20. And all the cars are the same?

> No!

Okay. So, what's the difference?

> Money.

I don't get it.

> Loser teams down the bottom spend about $150 million a year on their cars.

Really? $150 million. That's a lot.

> And the teams up the top spend about $400 million, Jason.

No, sir. That's just—

> Do that, Jason. Slurrrrrp.

But, sir. That's a big difference.

> Yeah! It is.

I don't know about this, sir. Maybe we give some of the teams down the bottom more, and—

> Give Ferrari $75 million.

Oh. Are Ferrari one of the teams down the bottom that need a bit of help?

> Pffffft. No, Jason!

So you give them even more money?

> Yeah!

What about the other teams?

> Nah!

Why not?

> Jason! You're walking a fine line.

Well, how much slower are the slower cars?

> About a second and a half.

Is that all?

> Yeah!

So an extra second and a half will cost you about—

> About $250 million a year. Hahahaha.

God. *Sigh*. What about the track?

> There are circuits all over the world, Jason.
> The driving teams travel to all sorts of countries
> to race on different tracks.

And a track is defined by?

> The white line, Jason.

Aha. Great. That's easy.

> Or maybe it's defined by the start of the curbs.

Wait, so—

> Or the back of the curbs.

So it's not the white line?

> Or maybe it's a little bit of blue paint.

Next you're going to tell me the track is defined by a wall or something.

> That's a good idea, Jason. The wall! *Slurrrrp*.

You don't think there might be too many definitions of the track?

> Don't be a Jason, Jason! It all depends on the
> track! Or how the race director is feeling that day.
> If he's done a poo that morning, or ... anyway, it
> changes, Jason!

Sir, these are cars that are racing at, what—

> Three hundred kilometres an hour, I know.

Sir, we should make the rules for racing the same for every single race, right?

> Hahaha.

Sir?

Slurrrrrp.

Right?

Hehehe. Jason, Jason, Jason. Formula One is like rhythmic gymnastics. You know the one where they roll over and throw a ball up in the air? Haha! We don't really know what's happening with the judges' score but what we love the most is when they drop the ball and fall over.

That doesn't make sense.

Shut up, Jason! Teammates.

Teammates, sir?

Yes, each team has two cars, Jason. So the drivers are teammates.

Ah, so there's, like, teamwork!

Pfffft. No, Jason! Every driver thinks that they're the best driver, and they would rather crash than be overtaken by their teammate.

Right. So, how does a race work?

The starting grid order is defined by who can do the fastest single lap time. And then, at the start of the race, they put five lights on, and when they go off, they start the race. And then it's all a bit crazy and everyone tries to not crash going round the first corner. And then the leaders who spent $400 million, they break away from the rest, and then they drive till the end and they win.

Sorry, so after the first corner they just race till the end?

Yeah!

Really?

> No, Jason. They can't make it to the end.

Why not?

> Because they've got crappy tyres that don't last the whole race. So they have to change them.

And how do they do that?

> They drive into the pit lane, and then 50,000 people run out and change the tyres.

How long does that take?

> Two seconds.

Two seconds?!

> Oooh, Jason. Make it so a car's whole race can be totally ruined by one guy who couldn't put a tyre on properly. Haha!

What? That's a lot of responsibility for one guy.

> Pfffft. Shut up, Jason!

Sigh. So, what else?

> Team bosses whinge at each other, the winners spray champagne in each other's faces, and if anyone crashes, it definitely wasn't their fault.

Oookay.

Oh, and Jason! Make the most prestigious race on the calendar the most boring one. Ha!

Hang on, sir. That's—
Gotta go, Jason.

But, sir, I have so many more questions. Who pays for all these races?
Cigarette companies, Jason!

Wait, sir. Did you just say—
Bye!

Make the most prestigious race on the calendar the most boring one. Ha!

THE GUY WHO DECIDES ... FOOTY

Hello, sir. So, Australian football. What are we thinking?

Make athletic blokes run around a massive oval.

So, they just run around the oval, like a sprint?

No, Jason! They chase a ball around.

Oh, like soccer.

No, Jason! Not a round ball. An oval ball.

Like rugby?

Pointier than rugby.

Like an American football?

Not that pointy, Jason!

Right. And what do they do exactly?

They kick the ball to each other, move it down the field and get a goal. Haha.

And what are the goals?

Massive poles.

Pardon?

Stick two massive poles at either end of the field, Jason.

Right.

> And if they get the ball through the massive poles they get—

One point!

> Pffffft. No, Jason! Six points.

Okay. So throw the pointy ball through the massive poles and—

> Jason, Jason, Jason. What are you, stupid? You don't throw the ball. It's called Australian football. You've got to kick it through the massive poles.

Right. And if you hit the pole and it still goes through, you get six points?

> Nup. You get one point for that.

And what if you miss the big goals completely?

> Give 'em a point.

What? No, sir, you should get nothing if you miss, right?

> Shut up, Jason. Let's put some smaller sticks on either side of the massive sticks, so if you get it through them, you get a point. Haha. Slurrrrp.

So you get a point for missing?

> Yeah.

Sir, this is very confusing. I don't think any other sport gives you a point for missing.

> Shut up, Jason! If you don't like this job, go and get another one. I'm sure you'd make a great poop inspector.

Sigh. So what if you hit one of the small posts? You get a point for that too?

> Nothing.

Nothing? Why? You said—

> Because they missed, Jason. What are you, an idiot?

Right. So if you're calling this football, you can only use your feet?

> No, you can pick the ball up and run with it.

Oh, I get it. You can run the whole length of the field and kick a goal!

> Pfffft. No, Jason! Every 15 metres, you've got to bounce it.

What?

> You heard me, Jason!

Bounce an oval ball?

> Yeah!

Sir, have you ever seen an oval ball bounce?

> Hahahaha! All part of the fun, Jason.

So, you kick the ball to a teammate—

> And if they catch it, they get a free kick.

So, that's a big part of the game — the catch.

> Yeah. But we're not calling it a catch. We'll call it a ... John.

Really?

> Wait! No. A Dave! No! A Mark! Yeah. Do that.

Right. And where do all the players stand?

> Six in the forward line, six in the centre and six at the back.

Okay, so like netball, they have to stay in those areas?

69

Nup. They can go anywhere.

No, sir. That means all 36 players could be standing in the one spot.
Yep.

Well, it's lucky they can't touch each other.
Tackling!

Oh, don't tell me. So—
Yeah! All the players can tackle each other.

Sir, this just sounds like a free for all.
Hahahaha! *Slurrrrp.*

This is going to be like a royal rumble. So, sir, we'll obviously have to give them all body armour and helmets, like in American football.
Pfffft. No, Jason! A mouthguard.

Is that it? But—
Jason, Jason, Jason. You don't have to do everything like America. It would be un-Australian if the players wore protection.

But they do wear mouthguards.
Teeth are important, Jason.

Sir, I think we should have some rules.
Fine! No tripping and no tackling above the shoulders.

Well, that's a good start, sir.
Ooh. A speccy!

What's that, sir?

> A spectacular Mark, Jason! When a
> player sits on someone else's head to
> take a catch.

But sir, you just said no contact to the head.

> Don't be an idiot, Jason! It's fine
> when you're taking a speccy!

Right. *Sigh*. And do you *have* to kick the ball?

> No, Jason. You can pass it
> with your hands.

Oh, so a throw.

> No, you can't *throw* it. That'd be a free kick to the
> other team.

Aha. And how does the game start?

> The umpire bounces the ball in the middle of the oval
> and two massive blokes run at each other and stick
> their knees into each other's ribs, while trying to tap
> the ball.

And how long does the game go for?

> Hours, Jason! Hahaha. *Slurrrrp*. Next!

Oh, that'd be rugby league then, sir.

> Easy. Have 13 players on each side, on a rectangular
> field, advancing a ball down the ground to score
> points.

Well, that sounds fun, sir.

> Running into a brick wall.

Sorry. What?

> It's like running into a brick wall.

I don't understand.

> What are you, an idiot? The team without the ball
> becomes a brick wall!

Right.

> And the player with the ball runs into it.

Umm. Is that it?

> Pretty much. Gotta go, Jason!

My head hurts.

MUSICAL INTERLUDE FROM THE BRIGHTON LADIES

Hello, darlings! Yes, it's time for a little sing-song. To the tune of, well, you'll get the idea. Hit it!

Darling I'm a rich girl, big-lipped yuppie in my X5, sipping on my almond latte

I've got Bobo in my face, drink Ruinart by the case, flashing my thighs all over the place

Sing it!

We aaare, we aaare wankers! Your turn!

We aaare, we aaare wankers!

Darling you're a young boy, strong boy, sitting in your seat come and clean my pool one day

You need super chic fits, some filler in your lips, play your cards right I'll show you my fake – ooh!

Sing it!

We aaare, we aaare wankers! Don't be shy, darlings!

We aaare, we aaare wankers!

Bravo, darlings. You're one of us now.

A MELBOURNE SHOPPING CART

Hello, Melbourne. I'm your shop assistant from hell. So, let's ring up these items of yours and see what you've got ...

Oh, a KeepCup. That's pretty fucking standard, isn't it?

Aha, organically and ethically sourced coffee beans.

Oh, almond milk. Yeah, could have seen that coming.

And soy milk. Don't know why you bother.

And oat milk.

And pea milk. Really?

Coconut milk.

Hemp milk. Don't you need a prescription for this?

Birkenstocks. Typical.

An umbrella. Naturally.

Craft beer. Whatever.

Oh, a sourdough starter. Gross.

A case of kombucha.

An invite to a random inner-north house party.

Masks. Yeah, probably a safe bet.

Oh, tickets to an underground jazz bar. Probably one of those places that you need a shovel, a map and a secret password to get into.

Crocs. You've gotta be kidding me.

An electric scooter.

A second-hand Subaru, with a Triple R sticker.

A fiddle-leaf.

A wine subscription.

What's this? A collection of vintage records that you'll never play. Yup.

Copious amounts of gin.

A VIP card to Savers. Ethically responsible, well done.

Oh, and a premium membership to ASOS... I won't tell anyone about that one.

An MCC membership you've been waiting 200 years for.

Oh, The World's Longest Lunch, eh. Two ... err ... *one* ticket. Thanks very much.

A morning jog around the Tan, like everyone else.

Oh, look at this. A full lounge set of overpriced mid-century furniture. Good on *you*.

An earring.

A moustache.

A mullet.

Sunburn.

A doughnut from the Queen Vic Market.

All right, I think that's it. Do you need a hand taking this out to your fixie? What's that? You'll just put it all in your rucksack? Are you seriously calling that thing you've got a rucksack? It's a kid's backpack. Calling it a rucksack doesn't make it any more adult. What kind of word is *rucksack*, anyway? It's got *sack* in it. Oh, you do, do you? You actually own a *hessian* rucksack? I think we're done here. Next!

A SYDNEY SHOPPING CART

Hello, Sydney. I'm your friendly shop assistant from hell.
Let's see what you've got in your shopping cart ...

Mild road rage.

The impulse to ask where someone went to school.

Two deceased indoor plants.

A towel for a cheeky sunbake at lunchtime.

A crapload of red wine.

The business card of a PT who you'll never call.

Some activewear that you'll never break into a sweat in.

A morning swim at Icebergs.

The Bondi to Bronte walk. Typical.

Six hours. Sorry? Yes, I know what that's for. It's for your morning commute.

A whole lot of overpriced housing. Ooh, it doesn't quite fit.

A friend who was in a commercial once and never stops talking about it.

Possums.

Rats.

Something that you think is a stray cat but is actually a giant rat.

Deadly spiders.

Cockroaches.

Wednesday trivia night tickets.

An appearance at the opening of a new hip restaurant for Instagram that you'll never frequent again.

An STC subscription.

A giant book of excuses as to why you're always late because, well, you always are.

A pair of Yeezys that you bought second-hand on Marketplace.

Tickets to the SCG, but only for when Sydney's winning.

An overpriced haircut.

An eyebrow wax.

A fat freeze.

Some Botox.

A face peel.

A diet trend you'll change every month.

Ooh, a trip to Sydney DFO for four hours. With two of those hours for just getting out of the damn car park.

Some friends who you always talk about catching up with but who live over the bridge, so you'll never actually see them.

Pancakes at The Rocks.

Overpriced wicker furniture.

A trip to the Glebe Market.

A car small enough to fit in the stupidly small car parks they have in the city.

Copious amounts of parking tickets. They'll go nicely with

the mild road rage.

Tolls.

Tolls.

Tolls.

More tolls.

Tolls.

An iPhone. An Apple Watch. Some AirPods. An iPad *Pro*.

A mild to moderate hatred of Melbourne.

An industrial-strength umbrella.

Ooh, a stylish trench coat that you'll only bust out for one week of the year.

A daily green smoothie, with protein in it, of course.

Copious amounts of vitamins that you take on a daily basis. Then wee most of them out.

Knowledge of a private beach you think is secret. Like the 600,000 other people who go there.

A weekend brunch at The Grounds.

Generic work drinks on a harbour cruise.

A tick collar for the dog.

And last but not least – ooh, this is a big one – debt.

There you go! Off you go, Sydney. Bye! Next!

SYDNEY SHOPPING CART

Tolls.

Tolls.

Tolls.

Tolls.

Tolls.

Tolls.

More tolls.

Tolls.

MEANWHILE IN AUSTRALIA: A HISTORY OF THE PANDEMIC

WORLD HEALTH ORGANIZATION: There's a pandemic!

NSW: A *what*?

VIC: What's a pandemic?

THE PM: Don't worry. The pandemic has not reached our shores just yet.

RUBY PRINCESS: Hiiiiiiiii! Honk, honk!

THE PM: Sydney, keep the infected people on the boat.

NSW: Nah, let 'em off. Let 'em mingle! Yeah! We'd love to see them. And they haven't seen their families in a while.

VIC: What the hell, Sydney?!

TOM HANKS: I-I-I got Covid in Queensland.

ACT: What the hell, Queensland? You gave Forrest Gump Covid?!

HOLLYWOOD: Oh, Queensland, don't kill him. We need him back!

THE PM: Everyone, in the whole nation, *will* go into lockdown.

EVERYONE: What *is* lockdown? I don't know what lockdown is. Do we have to stay inside for a little bit? Ooh, I know what we should do! Buy up all the mince. Yeah, let's just buy mince! Raid the supermarkets for mince! And stack our fridges and freezer with it, because mince is what we want. A mince-based dish every night. Maybe some lasagne, some bolognese, some chilli con carne and some beef patties. Oh. All that chilli con carne. We definitely need three weeks' worth of toilet paper, too. Yeah! Go crazy for toilet paper! What?! It's all gone?! What are we going to use instead? What?! Paper towels? But they're all gone too?! Wet wipes!

THE PM: The whole nation will work from home.

JENNIFER FROM ACCOUNTS, ON ZOOM: ...

EVERYONE ELSE ON ZOOM: We can't hear you, Jennifer!

You must be on mute, Jennifer. Check your settings! Try pressing unmute! Or is it the headphone jack?! It's no use talking, Jennifer, we still can't hear you. Don't just mash the keyboard! It's been 18 months, Jennifer! You should know how this works by now!

JENNIFER FROM ACCOUNTS, ON ZOOM: Sorry? I didn't get any of that. I think you were on mute.

EVERYONE: Goddammit! But hey, restrictions are easing. We're coming out of lockdown. Yay!

WORLD HEALTH ORGANIZATION: There's a new strain. It's called the Delta.

VICTORIANS: We're back in lockdown.

DELTA GOODREM: They've called it *what*? They can't call it that! No one wants an event hosted by The Delta. I'm going to lose all my gigs! Can't we call it the Shannon Noll variant?

THE PM: The Delta has not reached our shores just yet.

SYDNEY LIMO DRIVER: *Cough.*

WA: Come on and sing it with us! If there's one case of Corona, shut the border!

QLD: Yeah, shut the border!

NSW: What the hell, Queensland?!

VICTORIANS: I'm sure this current lockdown won't last long.

VIC: Err ...

WA: Bloody filthy Victorians! It's time to build the Westralian Wall!

TRUMP: Did someone say wall?

VICTORIANS: We're finally coming out of lockdown!

VIC: Victoria will be going into a snap three-month lockdown.

NSW: Sucked in, Victoria!

DELTA: Hulloooo, NSW! Hahaha.

THE PM: Get vaccinated!

NSW: Stay in your home and get vaccinated! Bondi Beach is closed! It's end of times!

VIC: You stole our vaccines!

NSW: Shut up, Victoria! Get vaccinated!

EVERYONE: Look, what we're trying to do is get

vaccinated, and we'd all been told we could get the AZ, and that Australia was going to *make* the AZ, which was great. Until it wasn't great, because no one could get the AZ, and then it was all, like, well, let's get the Pfizer, but then there was no Pfizer, and if you're in your thirties it's like, I'm just going to be locked out of society and I'm trying to make a booking but it's, like, 30 weeks until I could get the bloody Pfizer, and now we're all stressed out – if only someone had just ordered enough vaccines!

JENNIFER FROM ACCOUNTS: Hiiiii! Did someone say vaccine? Because I won't be getting one of those, thank you very much.

NSW: Well, that means you won't be able to go anywhere.

ACT: Or do anything.

JENNIFER FROM ACCOUNTS: Ummm ... I don't think you're picking up what I'm putting down. My body, my choice. Okay? I've been doing my own research, on Facebook, and I won't be getting a vaccine. And what are you going to do about it? Lock me out of society? Oh. You've locked me out of society. Oh, no. Hello in there? Hello!? Oh, that cafe does look cosy.

VIC EARTHQUAKE: Arrrrrgh! *Rumble rumble.*

VICTORIANS: An earthquake?! Are you *serious*?!

NSW: The people of NSW are coming out of lockdown, just in time for ...

MAGPIES: Us! *Swwwwwooop*.

VIC: Victorians, we're coming out of lockdown, just in time for ...

MAGPIES: Also us! *Swwwwwooop*.

VICTORIANS: Arrrgh! Magpies!

ACT: I think the whole nation will be out of lockdown before Christmas. That means it's time for—

TERRITORIANS: Beers, beers, beers ... Beers, beers, beers!

SOUTH AFRICA: Howzit, folks. Rhonda, put the rrrrhino away. Folks, I have some important news. Here in South Africa we have found a new variant. It's highly infectious. It's called ...

OMICRON: Hullllooooo. Hahaha. My name is Omnibus. No. Omnivore. No, wait. Oberon. Err. Omicorn?

EVERYONE: Oh, wow. We were worried about 50 cases. Now it's 50,000 cases! Arrgh! What did you get for Christmas? Covid. What did *you* get for Christmas? Also Covid. What did little Timmy get for Christmas? He got a bike, a basketball ring, some skates and Covid!

WA: We didn't get Covid!

NT: Oh, shut up, Western Australia.

SA: Yeah, shut up.

TAS: Shut up!

VIC: Shut up!

NSW: Shut up!

QLD: Shut up!

ACT: Oh, wow. Well, that was a little bit crazy. But I think that peak is over now that summer's coming to an end.

NT: Summer ends?

QLD: We're doing great up here in Queensland!

THE FLOODS: *Sploooooosh.*

QLD: What the bloody hell?

NSW: Also, what the bloody hell? Stop it!

VIC: Guys. Warnie died.

EVERYONE: What? Oh, no.

WA: Heeeyyyy! We're open!

VIC: No one cares, WA!

THE GUY WHO DECIDES ... PACKAGING PART 3

Good morning, sir. We have some more products. Here's your drink.

Oh, thank you Jason.

Champagne?

Not until I've finished my gin, Jason.

No, I meant champagne, as in how to package it?

Put a cork in it. And then put a cage around the cork, and then wrap it an aluminium condom. Yeah.

Oookay. Um. A lollypop?

Put a plastic wrapper over the lolly bit at the end. And then twist it up, halfway down the stick. And then glue the living daylights out of it, so that the kids have to wait an extra five minutes while their parents open it. Pfffft. Hehe. Pfffft.

Wow. Off to quite a start. Um. Shoes?

> Put some paper feet in the shoes. And then wrap them in some paper. And then put them in a box. And then cut a little hole in the side of the box. So the shoes can breathe.

Continental cucumbers?

> Wrap them in plastic.

And put the plastic wrapping on the Lebanese cucumbers as well?

> Pfffffft. Nooo! Lebanese cucumbers don't need protection, Jason! Leave them nude.

Okay. Um. Hand soap?

> Put it in a plastic bottle with a pumpy-pump at the top. And then lock the pumpy-pump down and put some instructions on the top that are not very clear at all. Hehehe.

Cling film?

> Roll it on a cardboard tube and then put a little sticker with a little arrow on it to keep down the end, but when you take the sticker off it just rips a big hole through 65 layers of cling film. And then put it all in a box with a razor blade on the outside. Hahaha.

Baby wipes?

> Get a rectangular plastic bag kind of thing, and then just shove all the wipes in there, with a little oval opening. It must be an oval opening! And when you pull one out, they all come out! Haha!

Raspberries?

A see-through box with a little pillow for them to lie on.

Toy cars?

They can go in a little box with a window on the side. And then put two screws into the bottom of the box, into some useless pieces of plastic, and attach them to the bottom of the toy car. So the kids can't play with the car immediately, because they'll have to go and get a screwdriver. Hehehe!

I see, sir. And—

Wait! Jason, I think I need a top-up.

Okay, sir. I'll have to open another bottle. But I'll need a bottle opener.

What kind of stupid person puts a cork in a gin bottle?

You did, sir.

Get a bottle opener!

Yes, sir. Here we are. There's your top-up.

About time. Where were we?

Pringles, sir.

Ah, put them in a really long can, with an opening just small enough so your hand can't fit into the bottom. Hehe. And then put a little paper seal on the top, and a plastic lid that's supposed to go pop when you open it but doesn't.

92

Oookay. And now, a ream of paper?

> Ah, paper is very delicate, Jason. You don't want the paper to get wet. So wrap all the paper in another piece of paper.

Of course. Now the last one for today, sir. Baby humans.

> Put them in a sac. And then put them inside another human. And plug them in, via a cord. And let them grow and grow. And then when it's time to come out, let them come out through a tiny opening. The kind of opening that would make you think, 'How the fuck is that gonna fit through there?'

Sir, don't you think we should rethink—

> Another great job, Jason. Now freshen up my drink, will you?

Yes, sir. Your phone's ringing, sir.

> Well, hand it to me, Jason. Hullo? Yes, this is the Guy Who Decides Packaging. Who's this? Canada?

Canada? Why is—

> Shhh, Jason. I'm talking to Canada. They need help with their milk. Are you there, Canada? Good. Put your milk in a bag. Yes, you heard me right. A one-litre bag.

Milk in a bag, sir? *Pffft.*

> So, here's the thing, Canada. You can put the milk in a jug,

93

but don't pour it into the jug. Just put the whole bag in a jug. And cut the corner off the bag. And then pour it out, using the jug, which has the bag in it. No worries. Call any time! Bye!

Good one, sir.

What idiots.

THE GUY WHO DECIDES ... BITCOIN

Hello, sir. Today we're making a currency.

    Stop! I'm empty. Another drink, Jason!

Sir, are you sure you should have another one?

    I don't tell you how to be stupid, do I?

Um ... no?

    Make it digital! Slurrrrp.

Right. So, no notes or coins or anything?

    Yes, Jason! Nothing!

Okay, but is it backed by anything physical? Like, what *is* it?

    It's a coin!

But you just said it wasn't a coin.

    Yes, it's not a coin.

Aha. So, a digital coin, but—

    Yes, Jason! What are you, stupid?

And it's actually got nothing to do with coins?

> Correct, Jason!

Sigh. So what should we call it?

> Bitcoin.

But it's not a ... anyway, how does it work?

> Like anything, Jason. It's mined.

Right. Like mining, as in digging things out of the ground, like gold?

> Yes, Jason! Why is that so hard to understand?

Because it's nothing, sir, but it's something. *Sigh.* What are you mining?

> Nothing!

Sigh. So, how do you mine it, then?

> With a computer, Jason.

Oh, like a computer game?

> Pfffft. Currency is not a game, Jason! It's maths!

Maths? Okay. Can any computer do it?

> Why not?

Right. So I could do the mining on my laptop?

> Pffffft. No, Jason! That's not powerful enough! High-powered computers will do the mining. They'll solve complex problems! And when they solve the problems, they'll get some Bitcoin.

Um, if Bitcoin is like a dollar, are there cents?

> *No.*

Right, so you'll have just one Bitcoin or two, or whatever?

> *No.*

Ah, so, um …

> *Just when I thought you couldn't get any stupider, Jason. If you've got 0.2 of a Bitcoin, then you've got 0.2 of a Bitcoin. If you have 1.5 Bitcoins, you have 1.5 Bitcoins. And so on and so forth. Simple!*

Sure. And how much is it worth?

> *It's worth what anyone will pay for it, Jason.*

Okay, so how much is it worth right now?

> *Right now, US$49,000.*

Wow.

> *No, wait! It just dropped to US$3.70. Oh, and now it's back up, to US$33,000. No, back down again. Ooh, and up again! Haha! Slurrrrp.*

Sigh. So it's highly volatile? Is that good for a currency? I would have thought—

> *Shut up, Jason! People are getting rich!*

Probably more people are losing money, but anyhow, where do you keep your Bitcoin?

> *In a wallet, Jason!*

But you said it wasn't a physical thing. How—

It's not a physical thing, Jason! You keep your Bitcoin in a *digital* wallet.

Okay. And how do you access that?

You get a big, long number, Jason. And that's your wallet. You also get a really long password. Haha. Slurrrrrrp.

What if you lose your password?

Hmmm ... let me think, Jason. If you lose your password, you're fucked.

So, that means—

It means what it means, Jason. You're fucked.

Right. So say you bought a pizza for, like, 18,000 Bitcoin when the price of Bitcoin was low, and then Bitcoin goes up and that would be worth US$50,000, and you've suddenly got, like, US$900 million sitting in your wallet, but you've lost your password, you wouldn't be able to do anything about it?

For once in your life, Jason, you are correct. Anything else?

Sigh. Ah, no. Nothing else. I think that's it.

Oh, one more thing, Jason. Due to the fear of missing out, everyone will want Bitcoin. And when they get it, they won't know what to do with it. So these Bitcoin minnows hold on to it for too long, and the price will plummet. And then they'll panic and sell out. And the Bitcoin whales will get richer.

That just sounds mean. But, yep, okay. I'll have that done for you by the morning, sir.

Goodnight, Jason.

A BRISBANE SHOPPING CART

Hello there, Brisbane. So I'm your shop assistant. No shoes, I see. No surprises there, right? So, let's see what you've got in your cart today, shall we?

A Gerni and a shovel.

A wide-brimmed brown hat that's the same colour as your river.

Sunscreen.

Activewear that you don't get active in but *do* sweat in.

The inability to merge into traffic.

Left and right indicators. Really? What's the point if you don't use them? I'll just put those back for you.

An esky.

A very large fan.

A case of XXXX.

General dampness.

Toad repellent.

The desire to go to the beach.

Mild anger at the fact that Brisbane doesn't actually have a beach.

The shocking realisation that you'll have to settle for the inner-city beach on South Bank. Yes, it *is* full of piss.

Sweat patches.

Twelve pairs of thongs.

Termites.

Toads.

Rats.

Bats.

Mozzies.

A great deal on spirits at Aldi. Oh, wait. You don't have Aldi.

A debt collector knocking at your door for all your unpaid Go-Between Bridge tolls.

A small flex to your Melbourne friends about the weather.

A jumper that you bust out when the temperature dips below 25 degrees.

A phone call to your friends because you're lost at the Ekka.

A giant eye-roll at people who've moved up here from down south, even though you're originally from Victoria.

A life jacket.

Overpriced air-conditioning.

The word *ey* at the end of every sentence, *ey*? You'd better grab a lot more of those.

A fully optioned four-wheel drive, even though you'll never go four-wheel driving.

The inability to get a takeaway coffee after 2pm.

An overpriced taxi home from the city.

Insect repellent.

Footy shorts you wear when you're not playing footy.

Anti-frizz hairspray.

Flood insurance.

A reflex to hit the unfriend button when you find out someone's from the other side of 'The Brownsnake'.

A night out that you can't remember in the Valley.

And that's you done, Brisbane. Next!

WE ALL KNOW ONE OF THESE FAMILIES

MUM 1

'Emerald, Jade, Ruby, Sapphire, Crystal! Get in the car! And where's your brother, Moonstone?'

MUM 2

'Porsche and Mercedes, go and find your sisters Kia, and Ferrari. Oh, and don't forget your brother, Bentley. And then get in the Commodore!'

MUM 3

'So we have three girls. There's Pepper, Ginger and Rosemary. And the three boys are Herb, Basil and Allspice.'

MUM 4

'Here they are. Say hello, kids. This is River, Ocean and Lake. And that's our fourth over there, Puddle.'

MUM 5

'So, we have 11 kids. There's Tim, Tom, Tegan, Tara, Tyson, Taron, Talon, Telisha, girl Terri, boy Terry and Tinkerbell.'

MUM 6

'Kale, Honey, Bran, Cocoa, Almond Milk and Banana. That's what goes in my smoothie, but they *are* also my kids' names.'

DAD 1
'Yeah, I got three boys. Zeus, Titan and Rocky.
Then one girl. Her name's Princess.'

And that's our fourth over there, Puddle.

THE TOP 20 THINGS PARENTS SAY

20
Look at me when I'm talking to you.

19
I *said*, look at me when I'm talking to you.

18
I don't want to have to repeat myself.

17

I don't want to have to repeat myself.

16

I gave up my twenties for this.

15

What's in your mouth?

14

Put some pants on and get your hands off your penis.

13

Life sucks. Get over it.

12

Don't touch the poo/spider/dirt ...

11

Don't *eat* the poo/spider/dirt ...

10

What part of you thought that was a good idea?

9

Where are your shoes?

8

It'll end in tears.

7

Get away from me while I'm drinking my coffee.

6

Did you pick a winner?

5

Did you flush?

4

That's not a toy!

3

Because I said so.

2

Why!?

1

Oh, for fuck's sake.

THE GUY WHO DECIDES ... PAINT COLOURS

Hello, sir. We've got a few paint colours to get through. And I have these handy swatches here to help us along. So, let's start with this orangey colour. What do you think?
Butter Chicken.

Okay. And this slightly different orangey one?
Julia Gillard.

Really?
Wait, Jason! Trump. Yes, that colour should definitely be called Trump. Haha. Slurrrrp.

What about this white-ish one?
Rice.

Sure. And this other white-ish one?
Semen.

Come again?
You heard me, Jason! Semen!

107

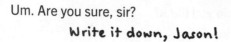

Sorry, sir. Yes, sir. What about this light green one?

> I'm thinking Crispy Lettuce.

Oh, it's already called that, sir.

> Fine! Call it Kermit the Frog then.

All right, I'll have that changed. And this light brown one?

> A Little Bit Like My Shit.

Um. Are you sure, sir?

> Write it down, Jason!

Yep, okay. Done. And this darker one?

> Ah, that's 100 Per Cent My Shit.

Yep. Okay. How about this?

> Bile.

Sigh. And this?

> Baby Poo.

And this?

> Pink Eye.

This?

> Garlic Naan.

And this?

> Menstruation.

Okay. I think that's enough, sir.

> Good. Another successful day in the office, Jason.
> Slurrrp. Well, I'm off to the pub then.

Right you are, sir. *Sigh.* I so need a new job.

Shortly afterwards, at a home-improvement store near you ...

CUSTOMER: Hello, could you help me out with some paint colours?

WORKER: Well, I *am* an interior designer. How can I help you?

CUSTOMER: I want my ceilings to be a white-ish colour.

WORKER: Of course, yes. I can see your ceiling covered in ... Semen.

CUSTOMER: Sorry? Did you say—

WORKER: Yes. Semen on the ceilings. And I'm thinking a little Bile on the walls. What do you think?

CUSTOMER: Umm ...

WORKER: Or maybe we go a little rustic. I really like this combination.

CUSTOMER: Okay. And what are those colours called?

WORKER: Well, it's a little Butter Chicken with Rice and Garlic Naan. Haha! Mmm.

CUSTOMER: You know what? I think I might try somewhere else. Thanks for your help.

WORKER: Oh, but you didn't even look at this one. It's 100 Per Cent My Shit.

CUSTOMER: I'm good, thanks, bye! Geez, who decides these names?

THE GUY WHO DECIDES ... CYCLING

Hello, sir. Cycling.

Hello, Jason. Make the bikes really light.

Oh, okay. And why?

So they can go really fast, Jason.

Cool. And where do they ride?

On the road.

On the road, with the cars?

No, Jason!

Why not?

Because cars would get stuck behind the cyclist, Jason. And it would make drivers really angry that they're stuck behind a guy who's pedalling his little heart out while the drivers in their cars can go much faster than that guy. That'll make drivers really angry, Jason.

Righto. But the cars *could* go around, sir?

And veer into incoming traffic, Jason? No, Jason!

What are you, an idiot?

Okay. I was just—
Wait! A bike lane.

A what?
It's a lane for bikes, Jason. Use your brain, Jason!

And where is this bike lane?
On the side of the road next to the cars.

Oh, that sounds great. So everyone will have enough room?
Yes, Jason.

So bike lanes are everywhere?
No, Jason.

Really?
Yes, really, Jason. And make the existing bike lanes full of crap, like rocks and pebbles and—

What? No!
... and shoes and bottles and sticks and overgrown plants ...

Sir, no.
... and a person and maybe some dog poo ...

But the bikes can ride over and around all this stuff, right?
No, Jason! The wheels on the road bikes are so thin that if the riders hit the smallest little rock, they'll go flying off their bike.

But, sir. Wait. Where do they ride, then?

The road.

But you said that's dangerous.
SHUT UP, JASON!

Well, I guess it's okay if it's just one cyclist on the road, yeah?
A peloton.

A what?
A peloton.

What's that?
Jason, Jason, Jason.
Cycling is a social sport, and people want to ride together. In a group ...

But—
... or a peloton. Hundreds of millions of cyclists in a group.

All in single file, though?
Not really.

Sigh. So what happens on busy roads?
Drivers of cars will lose their minds because they're stuck behind some cyclists and they'll think they're being delayed but lo and behold, it's peak hour, and the fastest way to get around is probably by bike and not in a car, which makes the drivers even more angry because every time they overtake a cyclist they get a red light and the cyclists just go pedalling past them again and the cars just have to overtake them again, and therein lies the circle—

No, no, sir.

> ... one big circle of angry. Hahaha.

Surely there's a better way, sir.

> Nup.

Well, what do these cyclists wear, sir? Something protective?

> Yes, Jason. A helmet.

And what about clothes? Motorcycle riders wear something protective. They wear leather, which at least—

> Lycra.

What?

> Tights.

Tights? Have you been watching *Robin Hood* again sir?

> Yeah! Full-body tights. Ha!

Very revealing. Are you sure that's a good idea? *Sigh*. So who likes cycling the most?

> Middle-aged dudes.

Maybe we should rethink this—

> Gotta go, Jason!

No, no. Wait. Please!

> Bye!

Where are you going?

> To the pub, Jason.
> What are you, an idiot?
> Slurrrp.

THE GUY WHO DECIDES ... RECYCLING

Ah, recycling, sir.

> *Borrrrrrring! Slurrrrrp.*

Sir, it's good for the environment. And it's the least you could do, with all that packaging you've decided.

> *Oh, all right then, Jason.*

So. What can we put in our recycling bins?

> *Trees!*

I don't understand, sir.

> *Jason, Jason, Jason. You have the intelligence of a turkey. No, wait! I really shouldn't offend turkeys like that. Listen very closely, Jason. Anything that comes from a tree, you can put in your recycling bin.*

Oh, okay. Like paper?

> *Yes, Jason. From a tree. Upstairs for thinking.*

So, in my recycling bin I can put wood and—

> *No!*

But you just said if it's from a—

Shut up, Jason!

Well, what about cardboard boxes?

Yep. Just make sure you flatten them, Jason.

Okay, makes sense. So cardboard cereal boxes are fine?

Yep.

Tissue boxes?

Yeah.

Packaging box?

Yep.

A box from the air fryer I just bought?

Of course, Jason.

Pizza box?

No!

But, sir. It's cardboard.

It's got too much grease and cheese on it, Jason!

Oookay.

Rip the lid off. Go with that.

Right. What about magazines?

Of course, Jason. They're paper.

Paper bags?

Yep.

116

Paper plates?

Pfffft. No, Jason!

But they've got the word *paper* in them. They're *paper* plates.

Too much food on them.

Err. Printing paper?

Yep.

Butcher's paper?

Yeah.

Shredded paper?

No, Jason!

What!?

It's too small. Haha! Slurrrrp.

But, sir, it's just paper, chopped up.

I said no, Jason. You've gotta put it in something so it doesn't just blow away, Jason.

I see. A bag?

Yeah!

Okay, great.

But also, no.

What? Why?

You can't recycle the bag if it's plastic, Jason.

A box, then?

A box.

But you'd prefer the box flattened.

> **Yes, Jason. I would.**

Okay. What about paper t—

> **Nup!**

But you didn't let me finish.

> **Whatever you were going to say, it's a no.**

I was going to say paper *towels*. It's *paper*.

> **It's too absorbent, Jason.**

Okay. What about cans?

> **Recycle them all.**

And what about—

> **Jason! I've got an idea!**

Oh, god. Here we go.

> **Instead of using recycling bins, people can bring their recycling to the facility.**

Right.

> **Haha! Slurrrrrp.**

Sir, why would people want to do that when they can put their recycling in a bin at home?

> **We'll give them money!**

Oh, okay, that sounds better.

> **Give them ten cents.**

Um … ten cents, sir? So I rock up to the facility with my paper and—

> **Pfffft. No, Jason! Not paper! Containers only.**

All right. That's still good. So it's 10 cents per container and I can bring along the container from my milk.

Not that.

What about a milk carton?

Not that.

An empty wine bottle?

Nope.

An empty gin bottle?

Slurrrrrrp. Not that, either.

Cordial bottle?

Nope.

A juice container?

Yes!

Finally.

Wait! Was it at least 90 per cent pure juice?

Umm ... yes?

Then, no. Not that.

Sir, it seems to me that people couldn't get any money for their recycling if—

Shut up, Jason! What would you know? People can bring their empty cans and bottles of booze from a big night on the turps.

119

So—

> And before you ask, no! We won't accept an empty bottle of mineral turpentine. So those people bring all their booze bottles and empty containers and then they get ten cents, per bottle.

But not spirit bottles?

> No, Jason! Not spirit bottles. They get their ten cents per container, and then they go on their merry way.

Okay, well, that's a really great incentive, sir. Sir? Where did you go? There's more on the list, sir! What about aluminium? Sir!?

MEANWHILE IN BRIGHTON PART 2

Darling, did you hear?

> Chantelle's implants are from Thailand? I know.

No, not that, darling.

> Well, what is it then, darling?

They changed their mind again, darling. About the Azeee, darling.

> The Azeee? Not the Pfiiiiizer?

No, not the Pfiiiiizer. The Azeee. Anyone can get it now.

Anyone? Well, that means that if people don't think we
look a day over 44—

Then they might actually *believe* we're not a day over
44, darling.

Oh, this is a wonderful day, darling.

Tony! Get the champaaaaaagne!

Oh, darling, and have you heard? There's a new girl at
yogalates.

A new girl at yoyo? Do tell.

Pandora, darling.

Pandora? Oh, it sounds like cheap jewellery. She had the
jab, darling?

Let's ask her, darling. There she is! Pandora!

That's Pandora, darling? Who's her doc? She doesn't
look a day over 39.

PANDORA: *Hello, ladies.*

Oh, Pandora. You look fab, darling. Who's your doc?

PANDORA: *Pardon?*

Your Bobo doc?

PANDORA: Bobo? No Bobo here, darlings.

Hahaha! No Bobo. Hahaha.

But you don't look a day over 39!

What's your secret?

Turmeric bath?

Shark cartilage?

Charcoal face scrub?

An avocado sauna?

Peptides?

Collagen?

A sea monkey bath?

Placenta face scrub?

PANDORA: Snails.

Snails!?

Snails!?

PANDORA: Yes. Snail extract ...

And it works, darling?

PANDORA: Well, how old do you think I am, darling?

Not a day over 39, darling.

PANDORA: Well, let me tell you, I got the Azeee.

The Azeee?

The Azeee? Not the Pfiiiizer?

PANDORA: Not the Pfiiiiiiizer. The Azeee.

But anyone can request the Azeee, darling—

PANDORA: I'm 69, darlings!

ohhhhhh.

No way.

PANDORA: Way, darlings. Now, if you'll excuse me, darlings, I need to go pick up some more snail serum from my vet. Goodbye.

Darling. This is a horrible day.

People could think we're not a day over 44 ...

But they could also think we're not a day over 69, darling!

What do we do, darling?

We just keep telling people we had the Pfiiiizer.

Yes, the Pfiiiiiiiiizer. I just can't believe she's had no
Bobo, darling.

I know. No Bobo?!

We need to go to the vet and get that snail serum,
darling.

Darling, I think she said semen.

Oh, snail semen. Well, that makes sense. Think of all
those active ingredients ...

Darling, I'll need another coffee.

Yes. Let's get another half almond, half oat—

Weak, strong ...

Three-quarters-full cup of chinooooo.

Chinnoooooo. Hold the chocolate.

But with two stevias, darling!

Oh yes, to die for.

Let's go, darling. Crunch.

What was that noise, darling?

Oh, no. It was a snail, darling. I trod on a snail!

Well, don't just stand there, darling. Get its semen!

MEANWHILE IN BYRON PART 2

Hey, babes

                                            Hey, babe.

Babe, can you believe we did a year of LD?

> Oh my god, I know. I mean, what a waste. Jo-Nathan
> says it was just a week of lockdown, but he's lying. It
> was a year, for sure. Mmm, look at that light.

Jo-Nathan! She's posing. Get pics!

> I can only hold this sad face for so long, Jo-Nathan. Now
> post that for me, with the caption: 'One year', with a
> crying face. No, wait! Make it the sad face. No! The one
> tear crying face. Make it that one. And hashtag Byron
> Bay. And hashtag influencer. And hashtag white linen.
> And hashtag vibes. And hashtag ... Chris. Actually, tag
> Chris in it. What's that? Tag Liam? Ummm ... I'll tag
> Liam next time. Ooh, and you've got to tag Lululemon.

Babes, are you working with Lulu?

Yeah, babe. But they don't have much cash.

Aw, what? No way. Is it under $50k?

Sigh. Yasss. What did you just say, Jo-Nathan? Are you even serious right now? There is so much more to it than just putting on free clothes and putting my picture on Insta!

She's right, Jo-Nathan. So many decisions to make. What's her hair gonna look like that day?

Or should I wear a hat? Just remember, Jo-Nathan, your job is to take the photos and look hot, both of which I can take away from you, okay? Now go and get us some boujee tea. Oh, and BTW, I'm booking you into that online photography course.

Thanks, Jo-Nathan. Make mine 30 per cent fennel, 80 per cent water. Yes, I know you think that doesn't even add up. But it adds up to me, all right?

So, babes, how's it going with that guy?

Babes, you won't believe it.

What is it? He followed you on Insta before you even met?

No.

Oh, no, don't tell me he's a frother, and he's stoked all the time.

No, not that.

Don't tell me he was the guy who dropped in on Chris at
                                           The Pass, was he?

That was so sad. But, no. That wasn't him.

                    Yeah. Poor Chris. So what *is* it then, babe?

Well, I found out where he lives.

                                           Get out, he doesn't.

He does.

                                     He lives in Suffolk Park?

Suffolk Park.

        Oh, babe. The median house price is only $1.6 mill in
                                               Suffolk Park.

I know. He was so cute too.

                          Jo-Nathan, you're back! Take a pic.

Get one of me, babe.

        The what? The memory card is full? Well, delete one,
                Jo-Nathan. Now hurry up, there's a cloud.

So, full moon tonight, yasss?

Definitely, babe. The sister circles are all booked out. And the post office is flat out sending healing crystals.

Yeah, but I wonder if they lose their charge in the post office underground tunnels. Yes, Jo-Nathan, I did say underground tunnels. How else do you think the mail gets into the letterbox? Anyway, babes, I've got to pick my car up from the White Range Rover dealership.

Oh, babe, we can drop you off. You heard her, Jo-Nathan. The White Range Rover dealership. Yes, that is what it's called, Jo-Nathan. They make White Range Rovers. Pardon? Other colours? As if, Jo-Nathan.

Babe, I can't hold this pose for much longer.

Jo-Nathan! The light is perfect! If you don't get this shot you'll be sleeping in the four-bedroom pool house!

Finally.

So, babes, launch parties this weekend?

I'm so there, babes. Free Stone & Wood.

And what are you going to do for your exercise today, babe?

Uh, I don't know. Lighthouse walk?

Jo-Nathan! You'd better have room on that memory card. We're going to the lighthouse.

PARENTS AT THE PARK: WHICH ONE ARE YOU?

THE LET'S BE FRIENDS

Hi! How are you going? Isn't this park the best? Which kiddy is yours? I've got six! They love it here. Do you want to be friends? I've got no friends. We should be friends. I love your pram. Where'd you get your pram? Beautiful day, isn't it?

THE VIDEOGRAPHER

Aw, you're going down the slide, buddy! Hang on, just wait! Let me get this on video. There we go. All right, go. Wait! Stop! Go back. Do that again! Now! Smile! Aw, he's having such a good time. You want to go on the swings? But I can't push you and film at the same time, buddy!

THE HELICOPTER

Watch yourself on those stairs. No, don't go near that, you'll fall over. Come on, hold my hand. We'll go up together. No! Not on the slide! Don't move! Stay there! I'll come down with you on the slide. It's so slippery! Keep away from that edge! Not on the pirate ship, no, not today. I'm coming, darling. Don't go up those other stairs without me! No, no, no, the fireman's pole is for over-18s. Not in the sandpit, darling! Who knows what's in there? Here, I'll carry you up the stairs. No, we're not climbing. I didn't even bring the rope and harness. Oh, you're playing in the tanbark. Come here, let's sanitise your hands.

THE INCOGNITO
All right, go and play. I'm busy on the phone. No, I can't look up, I have to read all these tweets. Are you pushing the other kids? If you're pushing the other kids, just stop it. Urgh. Whatever.

THE LET'S BE FRIENDS
Hiiiiii! Let's be friends!

THE INCOGNITO
Oh, god. It's THE LET'S BE FRIENDS. Please don't see me, please don't see me.

THE KIDULT
Hey, buddy, I'm right behind ya. Let's gooo! Race you to the top! Whoa! You found me! Let's go down the slide again! What did you say? Nooo, you don't want to go home yet! We've only been here three hours. And I'm having too much fun, come on! The slide again!

THE APOLOGISER
Sorry about my little one. Sorry. He's a bit tired. No, not down there, matey. Sorry! He's having a moment. Sorry, he's had a long day. Put that down, put that down. It's not yours! Sorry about that. Get back here. No, not that way. That's not your bike! Sorry, so sorry. Hey, that's someone else's lunchbox. Get out of that. Sorry!

JASON'S PARENTS
Jason! Get down from there! Jason, be kind to your brother! Jason!

I've told you. Let the other kids have a turn. How many times have I told you?! I've told you once, I've told you twice. Jason! Get off that swing now, Jason!

THE GRANDPARENT
They don't make parks like they used to. Back in my day, playgrounds were made out of trees. Like, just a tree. And that was it.

THE LET'S BE FRIENDS
Do you want to be friends? Anyone? Hey, that's a cute bag. Where did you get that from? Me and my six little terrors are just about to have a picnic. Want to join? Yeah, go on, sit down! Let's be friends! Oh, you're going? Okay, bye. Anyone else?

THE APOLOGISER
I *said*, put the poodle down. It's not yours. Sorry! So sorry. No, not up the slide! Sorry!

THE VIDEOGRAPHER
Just put this lapel microphone on for me, okay?

THE HELICOPTER
Don't touch the pole! It's got germs on it. Not down the slide, hun. It's got germs on it. Don't touch that. *Or* that. Okay, I'll lift you up there. But don't touch anything!

THE LET'S BE FRIENDS
Oh, isn't she the cutest? She'd get along with my kids, Jade, Amber, Crystal, Amethyst, Ruby, Sapphire and Granite.

JASON'S PARENTS
Where are you, Jason? Get here now. No. You've already had 15 lollipops.

THE HELICOPTER
Yeah, he loves this park. Don't touch that! He loves exploring. Wait for me! Don't go near there! No, wait!

THE GRANDPARENT
All right, now we'll go and get the biggest ice-cream in the world. Then hand you back to your mother and father, eh?

THE APOLOGISER
No, put the lollipop back. It's not yours to lick. Sorry! He's just tired. Sorry. He wouldn't normally. Sorry. Can you grab him for me? Thanks. Sorry!

THE LET'S BE FRIENDS
We could meet here again next week?! Or maybe tomorrow? Or this afternoon? Or just stay here now, together?

JASON'S PARENTS
No, I don't want to be your friend!

THE LET'S BE FRIENDS
Okay, bye. Next time, maybe?

THE GUY WHO DECIDES ... TIME

Morning, sir. Time today.

> Really, Jason? I don't have time for this.

What? What doesn't make sense.

> It will soon.

Okay. So what's first?

> We need something to measure time. Haha. Slurrrrp.

So what about something consistent, like the movement of atoms?

> A clock!

Right. And what does that look like?

> It's round and has numbers on it.

Okay.

> And it has some hands.

Hands?

> Yes, hands to point at the numbers, Jason. Slurrrrrp.

Great. I think I get it. So how many numbers?

> Make it ten.

Ah, a nice round number.

No! Wait! Make it 12.

Why 12?

You heard me, Jason! 12.

So, is that like a day?

Yes.

So a day is broken up into 12 segments?

No.

What?

Twenty-four.

Umm ... but—

It goes around twice, Jason!

So why don't we just put 24 on it?

Shut up, Jason!

All right. You're the boss. So we start at one, and—

No! 12!

We start at *12*, sir?

Yep.

Right. But you said it goes around twice, so how do we know which half of the day it is?

We'll start the day in the middle of the night. Haha.

Wow. *Sigh.* Okay. And so how do we read this clock?

The little hand points to the hour and the big hand points to the minute.

Sorry? It points to the hour? Even though all the hours aren't on there? Where are the minutes, then?

> All the way around, Jason!

Right. And how many minutes are there? 100?

> Sixty. Slurrrrrrp.

Sixty?! Of course. So I'll write those on there then.

> Pffffffft. No, Jason! What are you, an idiot? You have to guess where the minutes are!

What? How will little kids learn this?

> Some never will, Jason. Hahaha!

So when the big hand is pointing to the six ...

> It actually means 30. Yeah.

So six means 30. Great. Clear as day. So that's the clock, which is never going to take off. So, sir, remind me how many hours there are in a day.

> Twenty-four.

And minutes in an hour?

> Sixty!

And seconds in a minute?

> Sixty!

Okay. And I see you have milliseconds here, so I'll just put 60 milliseconds in a second.

> Errrrrrrgh. Wrong.

Not 60?

> Errrrrrrgh. Wrong!

136

Twenty-four?

> **Wrong again!**

Well, what is it then?

> **Jason, Jason, Jason. You get stupider by the millisecond ... of which there are 1000 in a second. Haha!**

Really?

> **Really, really.**

But how do we even know what a second is?

> **We measure it with a clock, Jason.**

Didn't you just make up the clock?

> **Yep.**

So how do you know if it's accurate?

> **We measure it with a clock, Jason.**

But didn't you just make up the clock?

> **Yeah.**

So ... how do you know ... if it's accurate?

> **We measure it ... with a clock ... Jason.**

But ... didn't you just ... make up the ... clock?

> **I told you I didn't have time for this, Jason! Urgh. Time to go!**

But ... didn't ... you ... just ... make up ... the clock? How ... do you know ... if it's ... accurate? But ... didn't ... you just ... make ... up ... the clock?

THE GUY WHO DECIDES ... KIDS' TV

Good morning, sir. Your drink, sir.

> It is a good morning, Jason. Slurrrrp. What have you got for me?

Children's television, sir.

> Sure. What have you got for me?

Umm, you're supposed to make up the shows, sir.

> Shut up, Jason. I knew that. What do kids like?

Dinosaurs, trains ...

> A dinosaur train. Next!

Okay. I think kids like monsters?

> A ping-pong ball show.

Ummm ...

> Get some colourful, shaggy fabric and shape it into monsters, Jason.

Is that it?

> No, Jason! They've got ping-pong balls for eyes and they've got really high, sweet voices.

Aw, that sounds nice. Do the voice for me, sir.

> I don't do impressions, Jason!

How is it an impression? You're making it up.

> Pfffft. Righto, smartypants. They'll sound like this: 'I wuv you, Mr Jason. Teeheehee.'

That is the nicest thing you've ever said to me, sir. I should have been recording that. So, what else?

> Make them all live on the same street.

Aww.

> And then shove an old man's hand up all of their arses!

Whoa. That took a turn.

> And make one live in a bin.

Right. Other ideas?

> Get some people to dress up in colourful fat suits. Haha. And make their faces look like they could be out of a horror film. Slurrrrp.

Remember, sir, this is for kids' TV?

> TV! Good point, Jason! Shove a TV in their guts!!

Umm. Does the TV work?

> Of course it does, Jason! They've got antennas on their heads.

Oookay.

> I'm bored now, Jason. Make them speak gibberish
> and let's get on to the next one.

Right. Well, kids love teddy bears.

> Get me a giant teddy bear, Jason. And give it a
> little hat, and a waistcoat, and a tie.

Sounds nice. What about matching pants?

> No, Jason! No pants!

Okay then. And how does this bear sound?

> The bear doesn't want to talk, Jason.

Oh, come on. Why not? It'd be cute. Give us another one of your
impressions.

> The bear's being kept in captivity, Jason. It doesn't
> want to talk.

Um. I see. Err. What's its name?

> Humphrey B Bear.

It has a middle name? What's the 'B' stand for?

> Balls-Out.

I'm not sure if that's really appropriate, sir.

> Gotta go, Jason. I've got to go and decide the
> weather. But here's the co-founder of the company.
> She can take it from here. Over to you, the Lady
> Who Decides.

Really, sir?

> Hello, Jason. Kids' TV, is it? Where are we up to?
> Slurrrrrp.

You drink as well? Great. Um, so I was thinking for the next one we could concentrate on laughter and fun?

> Get a man to dress up in his pyjamas and talk to an owl.

Well, that sounds nice.

> Give man an annoying high voice, like a cockatoo screeching. It's really annoying.

Right. And how do we do that?

> Castration, Jason. Castration. *Slurrrrp.*

Ouch.

> And just make him laugh all the time, Jason.
> And make the owl blue.

Okay. Have you got time for one more?

> Shut up, Jason! My time is very valuable. I must go and decide the weather.

You as well?

> You think it's a one-man job, Jason? You think the weather just decides itself, Jason?! You've got a lot to learn, Jason! Now, top me up before I go.

Sigh. Yes, madam.

THE GUY WHO DECIDES ... AUTOCORRECT PART 2

Morning, sir. So, in response to 'I feel like crap', someone is typing: 'Have you tried taking some *vocks*?' I think it could be Vicks, sir? What do you think?

> Dicks.

Err. How would *dicks* make you feel better?

> I don't know, Jason. People are weird. Slurrrrp.

Says the man who's had three drinks by 9am.

> Pardon, Jason?

Nothing, sir. Okay, I'll send *dicks*.

> Next!

Well, there's a lot of people just saying *fuck*, but I guess that's—

> No, no, no, Jason. They mean to say *duck*.

Okay. What about '*fuck* you'?

> Duck you.

'*Fucking* hell'?

> **Ducking hell.**

Sir, don't you think they actually mean *fuck*?

> **Pfffffft. Shut up, Jason! What would you know?**

Okay. This next one says '*fuck* a duck'.

> **Duck a fuck.**

Umm, sir, are you just replacing *fuck* with *duck* and *duck* with *fuck*?

> **Sometimes, Jason, you just need to shut the duck up.**

Sir, do you mean—

> **Duck! Yes, you heard me!**

Okay, sorry, sir. Here's another one: 'On way home, will just have sbags in bread for dinner for the kids.' Oh, I think they mean—

> **Shags!**

No, I was going to say—

> **Shags!**

But that doesn't make sense, sir. *Shags* in bread?

> **Bed.**

What?

> **You heard me, Jason. It should be shags in bed!**

Right. Well, those kids have an interesting dinner ahead of them. Better move on. What about this one, sir: 'I *lovr* you.' Well, that's an easy one at least.

> **Pfffffft. An easy one, Jason!? You think this is easy? Go on then, smartypants. What do you think it is?**

Umm ... I *love* you?

> No, Jason! It's not I *love* you. I'll sign you up for
> Married at First Sight, you're so stupid! It's: I *lube*
> you.

But, sir. They've just mis-typed it — the *r* is next to the *e*.

> Get out, Jason! You're done.

What? Really?

> Yes, Jason. Get out. I'll do it myself.

All right. Here's the phone. Bye.

> Stupid Jason. Gosh. What's next? Urgh. Stupid
> phone. I don't know the password for the app. I know!
> I'll text Jason. Here we go: 'Jason you idiot. What's
> the password!?'

Somewhere outside, Jason's phone buzzes. Cue a flurry of text messages.

> Jason, you IDOL!!! What is the ass word!!?

> > What?

> Twat? No, Jason! Twat is not correct,
> Jason!!! Ass words now!!!

> > Sir, I think you have to auto
> > cucumber these missiles.

> Stop speaking gerbils, Jason. Get back
> here now. I need you to feel up my ass!!!

> > Sir, I hope you mean
> > 'fill up my glass'.

> SHUT UP JASON!!! Get back here.

Ah, welcome back, Jason.

Hello, sir. Oh, um. I see your glass is full.
So what!?

So, ah … here's a message that might need some autocorrecting, sir. It reads: 'Get back here now. I need you to feel up my ass.' What would that be corrected to, do you think?
Hmmmm. That one seems correct, Jason. Slurrrrp.

Um. Are you sure, sir?
People are weird, Jason. People are weird.

Gulp. Oh dear.
Now fill up my glass, Jason!

Sigh. Thank duck.

Jason, I've decided I need a holiday. From you. I've been doing everything around here. And ... ANOTHER POST-IT NOTE, JASON! THIS TIME A BIGGER ONE!

Yes, sir. Here you are, sir.

Better. Book me a holiday, Jason. A nice Airbnb on a beach somewhere a long way from you. With fully stocked fridge and drinks cabinet.

Okay, sir. Are you sure you want an Airbnb? They can be hard to get at short notice. A hotel room might be—

I SAID AN AIRBNB, JASON! It's not a holiday if I can't swan about in someone else's house scoffing at their books and their art and their colour schemes.

I understand, sir.

Do you, Jason? Do you?

IF YOUR IPHONE WAS A PERSON

Who the hell are you? I'm not unlocking *anything* until I can see your face. Nope! Still not good enough. You'll have to use the passcode. Okay, good, you're putting it in. Oh, wait, I can see your face now. It *is* you. Open! Hehe. That was awkward.

Now, I'm just letting you know that I've got 20 per cent battery power left. So, I'm just going to turn that little picture of the battery *red*. So start stressing about plugging me in soon, okay? Thanks!

Oh god, what have you plugged into me?! I mean, thank you for plugging in this accessory but, I'm sorry, I'm just not dealing with *this* cable. It's not compatible. You clearly bought it from some shitty generic website. Get it off me! Get it out!

Ah, would you just look at me? I'm so beautiful. Wait, what are you doing?! What are you putting this cover on me for?! It's ugly. Yuk! What do you mean I'm fragile? How dare you. I'm not fragile! Argh! A rock! Careful! All right, all right, maybe I am a little bit delicate!

You what? You want to use that app? Urgh. Well, you have to download it again. God. You don't use it for three years and suddenly you expect it to work for you just like that. Just wait, okay? I'm still downloading it, *okay*? Stop trying to open me! I told you, I'm downloading it! Oh, and just letting you know, your storage is almost full. So, would you like to delete all of your messages, all of your photos, all of your videos or all of your emails? Ha. Didn't think so. I'm just going to go ahead and sign you up for an iCloud storage plan.

Nope, I'm not doing it. No! I told you. No way. Yeah? Well, fuck you too. Who in their right mind would want to listen to music and charge their iPhone at the same time, anyway? Idiot.

Listen up, apps! I don't care how long it takes. If you're open for a week, a month or a year, you stay open until he closes you, all right? Oi! And you! You have 5 per cent battery power left! So it's high time you plugged me in. *With* your official Apple charger. It's just over there, okay? Yeah, that one – the one that doesn't quite reach to your bedside. So yes, if you want to look at me while I'm charging, you'll have to hang your face over the edge of the bed.

Isn't it great that I have such an amazing memory? You don't have to worry about a thing, thanks to me. Like, I remember when you spelled GROCERY STORY in all capitals in 2010. So I'm just going to go ahead and replace that for you forever. You're welcome. GROCERY STORE. Hahaha.

Hey! You've got a message! But I'm not showing you any of the details until you show me your damn face, okay? Oh my god! Who is *that*?! I don't know that face at all! WE'VE BEEN STOLEN! Prepare to erase! Quick! Close everything and – oh … it *is* you? Bad lighting, I guess. Hi!

So, I see you've typed a little phone number in there. I've been snooping around in your emails. Don't quote me on it but I think this number is MAYBE JASON?

Everyone! Shake! He's moving all the icons around! Keep shaking! And remember, if he moves you to the side, he doesn't want to put you on the *next* page, he probably wants to put you on the fifth page along, okay? Haha.

I'm too hot! You're going to have to cool me down! My god, it's soooo hot. I can't – oh ... I'm better now.

Just plug me in, goddammit! I'm down to 2 per cent! I'm holding on as long as I can! Hey, battery! Have we got enough juice to finish this Facetime call? We do? Really? Well, I don't care. Stuff him. I'm shutting down anyway! Hehe.

INSPIRATIONAL QUOTES VERSUS KIDS' QUOTES

'In any moment of decision, the best thing you can do is the right thing ... and the worst thing you can do is nothing.' – Theodore Roosevelt

'I ate all my veggies! Also, I've done a poo in my pants.' - Kid

'Never give up on what you really want to do. The person with big dreams is more powerful than one with all the facts.' – Albert Einstein

'Have you been drinking again, Mum?' - Kid

'Winning doesn't always mean being first. Winning means you're doing better than you've done before.' – Bonnie Blair

'I didn't make it to the toilet in time! But I got closer than yesterday!' - Kid

'Every action of your life touches on some chord that will vibrate in eternity.' – Edwin Hubbell Chapin

'Dad, I killed a bird with a rock.' - Kid

'When you do the common things in life in an uncommon way, you will command the attention of the world.' – George Washington Carver

'Hey, everyone, I'm buttering toast with my poo!' - Kid

MEANWHILE IN BRIGHTON PART 3

Hello, darling.

Darling.

Darling, have you frozen up? Your face is—

That's the look I'm going for, darling.

I love it. Did you hear?

Hear what, darling?

There's a *pewwwp* rider in Brighton, darling.

A pewwwp rider? What's a pewwwp rider?

Someone who's pewwwping in our front lawns, darling. And what's worse, darling, is that—

Oh, no. Don't tell me. They're from Frankston?!

No, not that.

They wear Lorna Jane, don't they?

No, not Lorrrrna, darling.

Then what *is* it, darling?

It's a cyyyyyyyclist, darling.

A cyyyyyyyclist? No way.

Way.

A pewwwping cyyyyyclist? I don't know what's worse.
The pewwwping—

Or the cyyyycling, darling.

Oh, it must stop, darling.

They're bringing a bad reputation to Briiiiiiighton. We must act.

But, darling, don't you remember? We're busy with our
Bobo today.

**Oh, this is joyous news! We must drink before we go.
Tony! Pour me a Ruinarrrrrrt!**

Ruinarrrrrrt for me too, Tony!

One hour later.

153

Oh, that's sooo much better. Show me you, darling.

How do I look, darling?

Oh, darling. Once again, Dr Bill Oonlips has done an
incredible job.

Can you see any emotion, darling?

No.

Fantastic.

So, what are we going to do about the pewwwping
cyyyyclist, darling? He's ruining our Beach Road,
darling. Bring back the 5 kilometre radius, I say.

Darling, I've got it!

Oh, darling, this must be a good one. I can't see the
excitement in your face.

A bewwwwmgate!

A bewwwwwmgate?

Yes! A bewwwwwmgate at the entrance to Briiiiiighton!
You can't enter Briiiiiighton unless—

You're dressed appropriately? Have recently had some
Bobo? Have done a pewwwwp at home?!

No, darling. A Briiiiighton tax upon entry. You have to
swipe your platinum to get in.

A donaaaaation? Where does the money go?
The yacht club?

Yes! The poor people of the yacht club have suffered long enough.

And we do need that underground aquarium car park for all those X5s.

Damn right we do. As long as we don't have to celebrate at the club by drinking Moet & Chandon. Blerrrgh.

Oh, just the thought of it, darling. I hope you can't see the horror in my face.

Can't see a thing in that face, darling.

God, I love Dr Bill. So, it's decided. Let's get a bewwwwmgate!

Tony! Find out where we can get a bewwwwmgate!

Probably Bunnings, Tony!

We'll be on the cover of The Briiiiiighton Weekly, for sure.

I can just see it: 'They stopped pewwwp riders.'

Oh, darling. We need to get ready for that cover shot. I'll call Dr Bill.

Tell him we want the full fill, darling!

Tony! Quick! Another round of Ruinarrrrrt!

MEANWHILE IN BYRON PART 3

Ahhhhh, babes.

Look at you, babe. So chill. Sunrise yoges?

No, babe.

No yoges!?

Sunrise yoni sunning.

Babe.

Yah.

Why at sunrise, babe?

Everyone loves a sunrise, babe, and my yoni is not excluded from that.

Oh my god, have you seen this, babe?

What, babe? Another boho garage sale?

No, babe ... it's Chris.

Our Chris?

He's bailed!

Oh, babe. He always has to go back to Hollywood because he's, you know, a movie star. He'll be back soon.

No, babe. I think he's selling Hemsville.

Nooo. Jo-Nathan! What was Hemsville Hemsworth again? About $30 mill? Oh my god.

This is the worst news, babe.

I can already feel it, babe. There's a void, babe.

Jo-Nathan! Take a pic of my sadness! And hashtag 'our Chris', and 'bye Chris', and 'Byron vibes'. And hashtag 'who will fill our void?' And hashtag 'please don't!'

Hmmm. You put a filter on that, right Jo-Nathan?

Babe, he always puts on a filter. Like, Gingham, at 87 per cent. To show me at my best. Don't you, Jo-Nathan? Oh my god. Are you kidding me right now?! You forgot the filter!?

Babe ...

This is my brand, Jo-Nathan! Take it seriously. That's it. I'm booking you in for an online social media marketing course, okay?

Babe ...

What, babe?

Guess where our Chris is moving.

I don't know. Bondi?

No, babe

He's moving back to LA, isn't he? It's closer to work.

No, babe. It's The Shire

Seriously?

Seriously. Like, near Caringbah.

And Cronulla.

Como.

Sylvania.

Gymea Bay.

Babe, that sounds like an STI. I've got a bit of Gymea, bae, if you know what I mean.

Babe, he's going to lose his Byron accent.

Thor won't sound the same, either. 'Hi, I'm Thor! The Prince of Thunder,' or whatever he is. Errr-rrrr-rrrr. They do that, don't they?

It's terrible, babe. And The Shire, babe? How many times is he going to be breath-tested on the Princess Highway in Kirrawee?

This is such bad news for our Byron.

HIPPIES: Maybe you should all go with him. And then we can have *our* Byron back.

Sorry, we can't hear you! Are they trying to do smoke signals or something? What is all that in the air?

Babe, they're not smoke signals.

You know, if Chris is going, we need a replacement.

Yes, babe. Like, a big celeb.

Ed Sheeran.

I think there's, like, way too much sun for him, babe.

Oh my god, yeah. He'd need, like, a really big hat.

Zac Efron could come back.

                              Babe, what about Liam?

Liam Neeson?

                                      No, I mean—

Liam Gallagher? Eww.

                            No, babe. Liam Hemsworth.

Oh, him ... maybe.

                    Uh, let's just forget about for now, babe. It's
                            depressing. We need to move on.

Yes, babe. I'm going shopping.

                                    White linen?

Yah. There'll be heaps more out there now because Elsa's
moving out as well. I wonder if she'll have, like, a boujee
garage sale.

Jo-Nathan! Get the White Range Rover ready. We need
   to take some pics. Oh, and remind me to hashtag the
                 White Range Rover dealership.

Oh, look, babe! I just hit 900k followers on Insta!

             No ... way. That's ... so good for you ... babe.

Isn't it? Almost a mill, babe.

We should take a pic together to celebrate, you know.
                                    And both be in it?

Or you could just take one of me.

        No, I'll be in it. It's okay. You can just tag me.

Tag you? Um ... yeah. Here we go. Say cheese.

                                    Tofu Gouda!

Got it.

                                    Let me see.

You'll see it on Insta, babe. I gotta go. I'm off to meet
up with the other gals in the 900k club. See you, babe.

        oh, okay. Bye, babe. Don't forget to tag me.
Jo-Nathan! Get in the White Range Rover. We're
                        having a crisis meeting!

THE GUY WHO DECIDES ... PACKAGING PART 4

Busy day today, sir. Deodorant?

> Put it in a pressurised can. And make it sssspray everywhere.

What about deodorant that's good for travelling?

> Put it in a little bottle with a ball at the top. The ball rolls round and mixes with the deodorant, so you can roll it on whenever you want.

That sounds good, sir.

> And, Jason, the first time they open it, make the ball really stuck. Ha. Slurrrrp.

Okay. Zooper Doopers?

> Put each one in a plastic tube and make it impossible for anyone to open one without breaking a tooth.

Okay ...

> AND make the side of it like a razor blade.

A razor blade. Right. What about a whole roast chicken?

> Oh, that can go in a slim-fitting baggy thing. To show off the currrrrves of the chicken. Haha. Oh! And when you open it, let all the juice go everywhere. Yeah.

Okay. Minced meat?

> Put in a tray and cover it with see-through plastic. Hehe. Ooh, and put a piece of paper underneath the mince that blends into the mince as it sucks in its juices, so when people tip their mince out into their frying pan they most likely will cook the paper too. Haha.

Right. What about chicken breast?

> Put it in a plastic tray. And then put a little sponge underneath the chicken to suck up all the juices. And then when you pull the chicken out, the sponge sticks to the bottom of the chicken.

Uh-huh. Mustard?

> Put it in a cone-shaped bottle with a little twisty lid so you can squeeze it out easily. Then fill the bottle with mustard, and a little bit of water at the top, so the first thing they get is water. And not mustard. What's next?

Um. Food-handling gloves?

> Whack 'em in a box in no specific order, so when you get one, you get them all.

Tea?

Put a little teaspoon of tea in a bag. And then attach a string to it via a staple or something. And then, on the other end of the string, staple a little cardboard tag that tells you what tea it is.

But won't the teabag outweigh the little tag, so that the tag will just fall into the cup?

What's your point?

Um. Okay. Let's move on. Expensive tea?

Just put all the leaves in a bag. They just fucking get the leaves themselves.

Smoked salmon?

Put the salmon on a golden board. Make it look like it's glistening in the sun. Ha! And then vacuum seal the crap out of it. And add a little arrow that says, 'Peel this corner'. But you can't peel it. Ha!

Puff pastry?

Stack them up. Piece of pastry, piece of plastic, piece of pastry, piece of plastic.

Okay, sir. Stack them up.

And blue. The plastic must be blue. Then put them all in a manila folder and shove them in the freezer.

A peeled mandarin?

Jason, Jason, Jason. That's stupid. The mandarin comes in its own natural packaging. Why on earth would we need to repackage it?

I don't know, sir. Maybe some people want already-peeled mandarins?

> **Fine. Put them on a tray and wrap them in plastic. Hah! Slurrrrrp.**

Kids' yoghurt?

> **Put it in a kind of squeezy pouch thing, with a little sucky bit on the end, so the little ones can use it without any problems.**

I like the sound of that, sir.

> **And then screw the lid on as tight as you can, so no kid could ever open it.**

Oh. Okay. And last one for the day, sir. Pawpaw.

> **Put a loosely knitted foam jumper around it.**

A what?

> **I shouldn't have to repeat myself, Jason. A loosely fitted foam jumper! And now I'm going home. Goodbye!**

Oh, sir, the door is the other way.

> **So it is, Jason. So it is.**

165

THE GUY WHO DECIDES ... OLYMPIC SPORTS PART 1

Morning, sir. We're thinking of having a great big spectacle that showcases what humans can do.

> Wonderful, Jason, Let's start with something huge. A big-ticket event.

Like what?

> How fast someone can run, Jason.

Okay. How far?

> 100 metres! Haha. The whole world will watch that, Jason.

Great. And how long will that take?

> Ten seconds.

Oh.

> Maybe nine seconds.

Really? So, shouldn't they run a little bit further then?

Fine. 200 metres.

Okay.

And maybe 400 metres.

Right. So that'd still be all over in a minute. What about—

And 800 metres!

Nice. So we've got 100, 200, then 400 and 800. I'll just put 1600 metres down as well—

Pfffffft. No, Jason! 1600 metres is too far! Make it 1500!

But, sir, you were doubling the distance each time, so—

Shut up, Jason. You heard me!

Sigh. Okay. What else?

Throw a hammer.

Oookay.

And a spear.

Yep.

And a plate!

A plate? Errr ...

Oooh! And a heavy ball! Haha.

Right, so throw a heavy ball? Cool.

Not throw, Jason! Put.

So, it's how far you can *put* the heavy ball?

Yeah! Put that.

Sigh. Anything else?

High jump.

That sounds good.

Long jump.

Now we're on a roll.

Triple jump.

Umm. What's that?

People have to do a little hop, Jason. And then a Julie Andrews in *The Sound of Music*, and then a jump. Haha!

A Julie Andrews? Right. What else?

Let the people hold a big stick and then use it to launch themselves over a big fence.

Okay. I've got a few questions about that one. So—

Shut up, Jason! I've got another one. Slurrrrp.

Well, it can't be worse than jumping over a fence with a pole.

A 100-metre race, but with fences!

Oh, god. What?

You heard me, Jason. Fences. Actually, make it 110 metres for the men, and just 100 metres for the women.

Sorry, but jumping over fences? What's the point? Nobody ever does that.

Horses do, Jason.

This is for humans, sir.

> Horses! Let's make a whole section for horses, Jason!

No, but, sir. This is for humans, so—

> Horse ballet! Haha.

What?

> And horses jumping over fences.

So, a 100-metre or 110-metre horse hurdle race?

> No, Jason! Let a little kid put the fences wherever they want, in a sandpit!

Sir, wait, this is for *humans*, not horses. Come on.

> Jason, Jason, Jason. You think I'm the idiot but actually, you are the idiot. Because we're going to put a human on top of the horse, to go along for the ride. Haha!

Can we just get back to the ones with just humans in them?

> Ribbon dancing!

Ribbon dancing?

> Bowling ball dancing!

Sigh.

> Dancing with ten-pin bowling pins! Upside-down swimming dancing! Lifting heavy stuff.

Wait, that's a good one! A show of strength! What do they lift?

> A bar with heavy stuff on the ends.

Nice. And how do they lift it?

They lift it up to their shoulders and then they push it above their heads.

Great.

And we'll call it the clean ... and jerk. Haha.

Really? *Jerk*? Could we not think of another—

No, Jason! And there's another way! You lift it straight off the ground and then straight up above your head.

All right. And what's that called?

Slurrrrrp. The snatch.

Ummm. Sir. But—

Shut up, Jason!

Okay, sir. Let's maybe look elsewhere. So any other—

Put some feathers in a cork, Jason. And get people to hit it over a net.

Aha. And what's that called?

Goodminton.

Oh, all right.

No, wait! Badminton.

Err, okay. And what's the feather cork thing called?

Cock!

Hey?!

A shuttlecock! Hehe.

Okay, you know what? That's enough. Let's just—
> Tennis!

Sigh ... here we go. Tennis.
> Yep.

Oh, so that's it? Tennis.
> Yep.

No silly stuff?
> No, Jason.

Great. I'll put down tennis.
> On a table!

What? No.
> You heard me, Jason. See you tomorrow! Bye!

Jeepers creepers. Tennis on a table?
I think he's finally lost it.

171

THE GUY WHO DECIDES ... PODCASTS

Hello, sir. So, we're looking for a brand new form of entertainment.
Sure. Any old Joe talking about stuff. Slurrrp.

Yeah. See, that doesn't really seem—
Comedy, true crime, entertainment!

Okay, that's sounding a bit more like it. Kind of like Netflix?
Pffffft. No, Jason! It's audio only.

Right. So, like radio?
Yes, but shitty radio.

Sorry?
You heard me, Jason!

Okay. So, like a *mini* radio show?
Yes, but with no music.

Oh, you've gotta have music, sir.
Fine! Crappy, royalty-free internet music. Haha! Slurrrrp.

But, sir, you said that it could be funny? Entertaining?

> Yes, Jason. It could be those things.

Oh, great.

> But it won't be.

I don't understand.

> Jason, Jason, Jason. The thing is, every man, woman and dog will be able to make a podcast.

Oh, so that's what it's called. I don't see how this is a bad thing.

> Oh, it'll be a bad thing, Jason.

But, sir, we are creating it now. We can just change whatever we want.

> Pfffft. We?

Umm. Sorry. *You*, sir.

> You're getting a bit shirty for your own britches, Jason.

I don't think that's the saying, sir.

> Shut up, Jason!

Well, how many podcasts will there be?

> Two.

Oh, just two. Well, that's—

> Million. Two million. Haha! Slurrrrp.

I think you'd be creating way too many there, sir.

> Shut up, Jason. The only thing you've ever created is a headache for me.

I'm pretty sure that headache is not from me, sir.

> *Slurrrp. So. The overwhelming majority of podcasts have only one episode, which is all you need to lose the motivation to talk to your buddy about skiffle-boarding, or to interview that one famous lady who went to your school.*

Right. Well, maybe these podcasts just need to be available in more places, sir.

> *Jason, Jason, Jason. They'll be free and available just about anywhere.*

Anywhere...

> *And give each one a boring introduction.*

What!?

> *And ads!*

But—

> *Yeah! Every single one can be sponsored by a company encouraging you to set up a website. Haha. Or to send out newsletters!*

Sir, shouldn't people be focused on their podcasts?

> *Yep. But why not build a website?*

Okay, sir. *Sigh.*

> *Awww ... what is it, Jason?*

Well, sir, it all seems a little ...

> *Slow? Yeah. Haha!*

Can't we add another feature, sir?

> *Absolutely, Jason.*

What about having popular music on the podcasts, instead of just—
Nope.

Maybe make it so not *everyone* can have a podcast?
Nope.

Well, can we at least make podcasts really exciting, so people want to relisten to them?
Shhh. I've got it, Jason.

Here we go.
Skip 30 seconds!

What?! You mean make that an option?
Yeah! You can skip 30 seconds of the podcast whenever you want! And listen to it sped up!

What? Why?
You heard me, Jason!

What about the ads?
Skip 'em!

The royalty-free music bits?
Skip 'em!

The intros that people have spent hours and hours on?
Skip it all, Jason! Hahaha!

What would people actually listen to?

> Shut up, Jason. Make it happen. I'm going to the pub. Ha.

Okay, bye. *Sigh.* Great. Something you listen to for entertainment, but its number one feature is that you can listen to it quickly.

> Sounds good to me, Jason! See ya!

You're getting a bit shirty for your own britches, Jason.

PARENTS R US: IF YOU HAD TO PURCHASE FATHERHOOD

CHASTITY: Hello and welcome! I'm your consultant, Chastity.

MAN: Hey.

CHASTITY: Wow, don't you look cool? You'll be in for a shock.

MAN: Pardon?

CHASTITY: Nothing! Let's get started. We have a wide range of features and upgrades here. I think you're going to be thrilled with what we can offer.

MAN: Oh, great.

CHASTITY: Let's run through the starter pack, okay? So

with this deal, you're going to be the fun one. Like when you walk in the door, the kids will say, 'Daddy's home! Let's play!' So cute. You'll also get love handles.

MAN: Umm ... sorry?

CHASTITY: They come standard, don't worry.

MAN: I'm not sure I want—

CHASTITY: And let's see, what else? No sleep is also standard. So is looking like hell, and a coffee addiction. Oooh, now you've got a choice here. Did you want to go to the gym twice a year or play golf once?

MAN: Well, like, I have a gym membership, and I like to keep myself in shape, so I think I'll be able to go more than twice a year.

CHASTITY: Right. I'll just type a note in here ... 'when the kids are at school, would like to go to the gym, often.' There you go, so—

MAN: Wait. School? That'd be, like, six years away at least ...

CHASTITY: Yah. Now, can you sneeze for me?

MAN: Huh?

CHASTITY: Sneeze. Just give me a sneeze if you could.

MAN: Oh, okay. Um ... *ah choo.*

CHASTITY: Right. I'm just going to add the extremely loud, completely over-the-top Dad Sneeze to your package here. There you go. Now, dad jokes. Thoughts?

MAN: Actually, yeah. So I know a lot of dads go with that whole *dad joke* thing. But I find it a bit, like, cringe, you know? So let's just leave that one out, yeah? It's just not me.

CHASTITY: Well, Mr Salty – am I saying that correctly? *Salt-ee*?

MAN: Yes.

CHASTITY: See, the thing is, Mr Salty, in this industry some things are just out of our hands, you know? We've got rules and regulations. I know, rules and regulations, *yuk*, right? Ha! But, look, some things *do* come standard and they have to be included in these packages. And dad jokes *is* one of those. So, would you like to have a read of the requirements? Here you go ...

MAN: Um. I guess I'll take a look. Hmmm. Oh. So, it says here when answering the phone, one must say 'y'ello'.

CHASTITY: 'Y'ello!' Classic, right?

MAN: Right. And I see it's got an example dad joke

here. 'What do you call a factory that makes okay products? A satisfactory.'

CHASTITY: Hahaha. But that's enough of that. I've only got so many fake laughs in me. Okay, so we're almost done. On a scale of one to ten, how much ear hair do you want?

MAN: Umm, sorry, but according to the form here, the only options I can tick are eight, nine or ten?

CHASTITY: Yeah, I know. Which one?

MAN: Um ... eight?

CHASTITY: And nose hair?

MAN: Um ...

CHASTITY: Eight it is. What about dorkiness?

MAN: This isn't fair, I—

CHASTITY: Eight.

JEFF: Hey, Chastity!

CHASTITY: Oh, that's just my colleague, Jeff. He's a father of three. Yes, Jeff, what is it?

JEFF: Did you hear that a book fell on my head the other day?

CHASTITY: Get out, no way!

JEFF: Yeah, I've only got my *shelf* to blame! HAHAHA!

CHASTITY: Ahaha. Good one, Jeff.

MAN: *So* cringe. Is that really what I'm going to be like when ...

CHASTITY: Yeah. Now, just a few more things. You'll start getting obsessed with your lawn, technology will start getting away from you a little bit, and you'll really begin to reflect on just how hard you had it as a kid. How are we feeling?

MAN: Umm ...

CHASTITY: Ooh, I forgot to mention, you'll start to grunt when you sit down, or stand up.

MAN: But, I'm—

CHASTITY: Thanks, Mr Salty! So, just to be clear, no returns, no cooling-off period and ... we're done!

MAN: Um. Okay. Err, *cheerio*, then.

CHASTITY: That's a great start. Good luck!

EXPLAINING JOBS LITERALLY: WHICH ONE ARE YOU?

Barista
Hey there, I'm a milk spinner. I spin milk.

Plastic Surgeon
I'm a face inflater.

Personal Trainer
I'm a tell-people-to-take-heavy-things-off-a-shelf-and-then-put-them-back-where-they-were instructor.

Real Estate Agent
I'm a tell-the-buyer-they-need-to-spend-more-money-and-tell-the-seller-to-take-what-they-can-get-erer.

Teacher
I'm a lose-my-voice-trying-to-control-your-entitled-kids-anator.

Butcher
I'm an animal deconstructor.

Fireman
I'm an office-building burnt-toast and false-alarm attender. Oh, and fire-putterer-outerer.

Removalist
I'm angry.

Concreter
I'm also angry.

Plumber
I'm a shit whisperer.

Parent
I'm just really, really tired.

I'm a lose-my-voice-trying-to-control-your-entitled-kids-anator.

BEFORE KIDS/ AFTER KIDS

Before

Yeah, we've decided it'll be all wooden toys in our house. No plastic whatsoever.

After

All right, fine! Get the plastic car tracks. As long as we can leave Kmart *this bloody instant*!

Before

Oh, I won't need to repeat myself. We'll be raising good little kiddies who respect our boundaries, and vice versa.

After

If I have to say it one more time … Don't make me say it again! How many times do I have to tell you?!

Before

Oh, we'll be dressing our kids super cool. And there are just so many beautiful outfits too. I love the earth tones. That's what we'll be going with.

After

You've worn that hideous little Peppa Pig T-shirt for the last three months! Fine. Wear it again.

Before
It's important to keep a routine for us adults too, so yeah, I'll still be going to the gym as a parent.

After
Mercedes! Pass me the chips! I can't move off this couch.

Before
Oh, for sure, our little fur baby here will still be our little princess. Kids won't change that.

After
Get that fucking dog outside!

Before
We think it's really important to give each parent some guilt-free alone time.

After
No, it's fine, you go and do the supermarket shopping. I'll just be here.

Before
We'll *always* be spontaneous and romantic, no matter what.

After
So sex is on Wednesday at 7:05pm, just after the kids have gone down. Put it in my iCloud.

Before

We'll teach our kids that they have to play in their rooms until 7:30am, *then* they can come and say good morning.

After

It's 5:15am, they're hungry, get up!

Before

They'll just eat the food they're given.

After

Porsche, your Weet-Bix is on the table! Holden, the battered fish with the batter taken off is waiting for you on the couch. And Mercedes, your duck à l'orange with potatoes dauphinoise is up at your highchair. And yes, I'll get the tomato sauce.

Before

Kids don't need screens. We never had them ...

After

Where's the TV remote? No, not that remote, the other remote with the 24-hour kids' TV network. What's that, kiddo? Yes, you can use my phone. Oh, and happy two-month birthday to you, little one ... it's an iPad!

Before

It's okay for kids to be bored. They'll just find something to do using their imaginations.

After

Here's a new plastic toy. Go and use your imagination.

Before
Routine, routine, routine. That's what it's all about. Dinner, bath, pyjamas, teeth, story, sing a song, sleep. It's simple, really.

After
Did you finish your dinner or feed it to the dog? Fine, we *won't* have a bath tonight. Stop biting on the toothbrush! No, 25 stories is enough. Okay, fine, we'll read it again. No, I didn't skip any pages! Come on, it's bedtime! Yes, I'll do 'Twinkle, Twinkle', but only for another two hours. But if you don't go to sleep after that, I'll burn all your plastic toys.

Before
I'm sure the little munchkin will be smart like me.

After
Great, so he's stubborn like me.

Before
My kid will be a respectable human, the kind who would never have a tantrum in public.

After
Just ignore him and wheel your shopping cart around him. Yeah, he throws these tantrums all the time.

Before
It's really important to follow through on discipline.

After
Young lady, if you don't get in the car this instant, I *will* be on the first mission to Mars and I *will* help colonise that planet *without* you! It's your choice. I'm serious. I'm calling Elon Musk now!

THE GUY WHO DECIDES ... DR GOOGLE DIAGNOSES

Hello, sir. Here's your drink. Today you'll be diagnosing people based on the symptoms they search online.

> Cancer.

But, sir, you haven't heard any of the symptoms yet. People are typing them in as we speak, so you should probably wait to hear the symptoms, yeah?

> Death!

Sir, you need to hear what people are suffering from before you—

> You're such a buzzkill, Jason. Urgh. Tell me the symptoms then. Slurrrrrp.

Let's see. Here's one. An itchy eye.

> Hmmm. They need a colonoscopy, Jason.

What's a colonoscopy got to do with an itchy eye!?

> Pfffft. Are you questioning my authority, Jason!? It's a brown eye, you idiot!

Right, sorry, sir. I should have known. Okay. The next one is an itchy *bottom*.

That's a symptom of being dead, Jason.

Sir, they're still typing their symptoms in, so I don't think they're dead.

Yeah. They're about to type, 'also one of my symptoms is that I'm dead.'

Ookay. We'll move along. What about this one: smelly gas?

Pull their wisdom teeth out, Jason.

Um. Are you sure?

Shut up, Jason! You heard me. Slurrrrp. Jason, are they new glasses?

Oh, yes, they are, sir. Dr Google said I needed them.

Huh. Did he now? Well, you look like even more of an idiot. What's next?

Um, thanks. Stiff joints?

Ah, that will be caprine arthritis encephalitis, Jason.

But, sir, that's only found in goats.

It must be a fucking goat then, Jason!

Right. How about this one then: a dry mouth?

Athlete's foot.

What? How would they get that?

Foot in mouth, Jason. Foot in mouth.

Okay, sir. Ringing in the ears. Ooh, I think
that's called t—
> Tetanus!

No, no, I was going to say t—
> Transit tetany!

That's only found in cows, sir.
> It doesn't say they're
> vegetarian, does it,
> Jason?

Umm ...
> Just put it down as
> the bubonic plague and move on, Jason.

Pain in the forearm. Could be tennis elbow?
> Pfffffft. Jason, Jason, Jason. Nobody has four
> arms. So it must be an octopus. With a rare case of
> wankery-too-much-itis. Slurrrrrp.

I *really* need a new job.
> Didn't catch that, Jason.

Um. Red hair?
> Amputate!

Amputate what?
> The hair, Jason!

A very large pimple.
> Chop it off.

Broken fingernail?

> Amputate the hand.

Sore knee?

> Amputate!

A headache?

> Lop it off at the neck!

A runny nose? Let me guess. Amputate.

> Pffffft. No, Jason! It's probably just a cold.
> Slurrrrrp. Or Ebola.

An arm twitch?

> Pregnant.

But it's a man, sir.

> Well, it's a pregnant man then, Jason.

Yeah. That seems—

> But it's unfortunate, Jason. Because he also has
> Ebola.

Um. And this one: lethargic?

> Man flu.

Ah, but see *that* symptom is from a woman, sir.

> Well, there you have it then, Jason. A pregnant
> man, and a woman with man flu. Haha!

Hang on, she's typing another symptom, sir.

> Interesting. What is it, Jason?

Headache. Urgh. Here we go.

> Off with her head, Jason! And just tell the rest of them that they all need lobotomies. Haha. I've got to go home now, Jason. Toodles.

Bye, sir. *Sigh*. Never a dull moment. Hmm. My shoulder's feeling a bit achey. I wonder what that might be. I'll Google it. Let's see … sore … shoulder … treatment. It says here that the treatment for a sore shoulder is a sore shoulder? That makes no sense. I wonder—

> It's a typo, you idiot! Saw shoulder! Hahahaha!

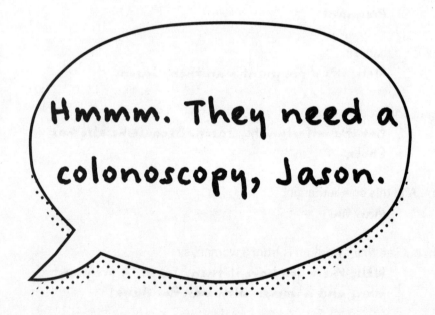

THE GUY WHO DECIDES ... HOROSCOPES

Good morning, sir. Here's your drink, sir. We're doing star signs. Let's start with Aries.

> Aries. Slurrrrp. On some days, but no specific days, you'll blink more often than other days.

Um. Is that it?

> And, this year for you will be like a piece of Blu-Tack holding up a picture, moments away from falling off the wall and smashing into a million pieces. Haha! Perhaps, you should have bought a hooker.

Don't you mean a hook, sir?

> You heard me, Jason! Hooker! What's next?

Okay. Let's do Taurus?

> Oh, yes. The moon is moving into the nebula copia thing, and that means that on Saturdays, you're going to go to the pub and get absolutely wasted and not remember anything in the morning until you have a bit of a vom and then you'll see that you ate carrot.

Sooo … every person who's a Taurus is going to get wasted on every Saturday of the whole year?

> Yes, Jason! And they should buy a lottery ticket, because their lucky numbers are 1, 2, 0 and 4000.

I don't think 0 is in the lottery, but sure, okay. Gemini?

> The stars … slurrrrrrp … are telling me that Geminis will have good luck this year. Haha! So, go and get a bow and arrow and fire it straight up into the air. And hopefully you'll get a duck for dinner.

Right. So—

> And, every Gemini who goes to the shops, they're going to get a parking spot. If they wait long enough. And if they don't wait long enough, they probably won't get one.

Aha. And Cancer?

> Shhh, Jason! I need a closer look at Cancer. Give me those glasses of yours!

Err. There you go, sir.

> My gosh, these are strong glasses. I can see right into Uranus! Slurrrrrp. This year, Cancerians need to buy two left shoes, and always turn left. Because turning right, although it says that it's right, is actually wrong. So, always turn left.

Always? What if they're in a car, sir? Do they still always turn left? Because that—

> Like a wise person once said, Jason, the cat chasing its tail is like the donkey whose tail is being used for Pin the Tail on the Donkey. What's next? Slurrrrp.

Yes, let's move on. Um, Leo?

> The stars are telling me herpes, Jason. Herpes.

Err. Sorry?

> Jason, Jason, Jason. Don't you get it? Every Leo will have herpes this year. So everybody else, I'd steer clear of Leos, if I was you. Slurrrrp.

Really?

> Shut up, Jason! What's next?

Virgo.

> For Virgos, one's first impulse might be to say exactly what's on their mind. But let's go with our *third* impulse. The one where you spend all your money on useless crap.

Right. Libra?

> Going on your morning jog and stepping in dog poo will bring you good luck. But *speaking* will bring you bad luck. So make your choices wisely! Slurrrrrp.

Scorpio?

> People can take the sole off the bottom of your shoe, but they can't take your heart. Unless they're a surgeon. Then they can probably take your heart. Haha! So, be careful who you meet. This year.

Okay. Umm ...

> And, do something with your hair, because it's ugly.

Sagittarius?

> God, there's more? Always have eyes in the back of your throat.

Did you mean eyes in the back of your head?

> Shut up, Jason! You heard me! Oooh, and an old lover from years gone by will reappear in your life. Or maybe they won't. Haha. *Slurrrrrp.*

And Capricorn?

> No one cares about you.

Oh, righto. That seems especially cruel, sir. So—

> I'm talking about all Capricorns, Jason! Nobody cares about them! I'm not talking about you!

It's just that—

> Ah, you're a Capricorn. Of course. Let's move on!

Sigh. Aquarius?

> Neptune and the Sagittarian are morphing to create babies. Well done. You will be expecting babies this year. All of you. Oh, and your ears smell. So clean them.

Okay. All Aquarians' ears smell.

> I was talking about you, Jason! Your ears stink.

Really? Oh. Um, so last one … Pisces?

> *Slurrrrrp.* Stepping on a nail can sometimes prick. But stepping on a prick can be the nail in the coffin. Did you get all that?

Does it really matter, sir?

> Bye, Jason!

THE GUY WHO DECIDES ... PARKING SIGNS

Morning, sir. You have a drink already, I see.

Delicious, Jason.

Okay, so people would like to park their cars in busy streets, sir.

Well, put up a sign to let them know where the ticket machine is, Jason.

Righto.

And have a little arrow pointing to exactly where the ticket machine will be.

Great, and all the information about when and when you can park will be on the machine?

No, Jason! We'll put a sign above that other sign that says you can park for one hour from 7:30am to 6:30pm.

Oh, good. That's plenty of time to park.

On a Sunday. Haha.

So ... just on a Sunday?

And only to the right of the sign.

What about to the left of the sign?

I haven't decided yet, Jason!

So, people who do park there on a Sunday have to get a ticket from the machine?

Pfffft. No, Jason! You don't need a ticket on a Sunday!

Sigh. All right. What's next?

Monday to Saturday, two-hour parking.

Both sides of the sign?

No!

To the left?

No!

To the right

Yes!

Okay. Monday to Saturday, two-hour parking—

Between the hours of 6:30 and 8:30.

Well, that's plenty of time!

PM, Jason. Haha!

Wait, what?

You heard me, Jason!

So, it's a two-hour park, with only a two-hour window.

Monday to Saturday. Yeah! Slurrrrrp.

No ticket required from the machine?

A ticket!

Sigh.

> And above that sign, put another sign.

Oh, god.

> One-hour parking 9:30am to 6:30pm, Monday to Friday. *Slurrrrp.*

Ummm ...

> And 7:30am to 6:30pm, one-hour parking, on a Saturday.

Sir, isn't this getting—

> And you'll need a ticket from the machine, Jason.

Okay. Right. Whew. Is that all?

> *Pffffft.* No, Jason! Put another sign on the top, saying 'No parking ever from 7:30am to 9:30am, Monday to Friday'!

Right. And have you decided yet about parking to the left of the sign?

> No stopping, ever! Except for buses that want to sit there for 25 minutes. Yeah. *Slurrrrrrp.*

Sigh. And what else?

> Jason, Jason, Jason. That's all. We don't want to confuse anyone.

Of course not, sir. It's just that, the other day I saw some of your other parking sign work, sir.

> Some of my finest, Jason.

And so I'm wondering if maybe you could help me out. I could give you a time and a day, and you could just tell me if I can park there or not. What do you think?

>Oh, I suppose so, Jason.

Right then. How about 8am, on a Monday?

>Fine.

Oh, good.

>No, Jason. I mean you'll get a fine.

Ah. And what about to the left of the sign, Wednesday, 3:30pm?

>Fine.

Right of the sign, 9am?

>Fine.

How about 10am?

>Fine.

Hang on, but the sign says—

>Pfffft. I said it's fine, Jason!

It's just a little confusing with you saying fine, and *fine*. What about right of—

>Fine!

But I didn't finish—

>Fine!

I was—

>Fine!

What!?

Fine!

Sir, if you do that one more—

Fine! Fine! Fine!

Okay! Stop! What about this one. Tuesday, *2am*, right of the sign, one-hour park. Hey? How about that one, sir?

Hmmm ... 2am. Tow away!

What?! Why?! It's 2am!

Special event, Jason. Haha. Slurrrrrp.

Oh, for farrr—

Indecent language, Jason! That's a fine!

Where are you going, sir?

To move my car, Jason!

AN ADELAIDE SHOPPING CART

Oh, Adelaide. Hi. I'm your checkout person with attitude. Let's see what you've got in your shopping cart, shall we?

Subtitles. No, I know they're not for you. They're for everyone who's not from Adelaide.

The Grand Prix. Oh, sorry, Melbourne's got that.

A strange accent that's 99 per cent bogan, with 1 per cent Queen's English, which comes out when you say words like *daaahnce* or *chaaahnce*.

The phrase 'heaps good'. Yeah, you'll need a few of those.

Some Lego. Sorry, *Lay*-go. Really? That's just weird.

A water filter, because your water tastes like a swimming pool.

A Holden bucket hat.

Trackies.

A mullet.

A Crows jersey.

Or a Port jersey.

A hatred of the person who's wearing the Port jersey.

A hatred of the person who's wearing the Crows jersey.

Jubilation over the fact that Adelaide was voted the most liveable city in Australia.

The fact that you still have to justify to everyone else why Adelaide is actually a good place to live.

Serial killers. Oh, that's quite a few you have there.

A proportionate fear of barrels.

A box of complaints about how far away something is if it's more than a 25-minute drive.

Reminding people when Sia comes up in conversation that *she's* from Adelaide.

A street directory. Yeah, you probably won't need that.

A windbreaker, because everywhere is a wind tunnel.

A random weird smell, which makes you wonder about where it's coming from, until you realise it's the River Torrens.

Telling yourself you'll never say, 'Let's meet at the Mall's Balls.'

The realisation that when you're meeting someone in Adelaide, the best place to meet actually is the Mall's Balls.

Some anger, due to the power failure that happens in that week in summer when it's 49 degrees.

A moderate to high hatred of Melbourne.

Cakes.

Honey ice cream.

Haigh's chocolate.

Farmers Union Iced Coffee.

An e-scooter.

A schooner that's actually a pot.

A pint that's actually a schooner.

An *imperial* pint that's actually a pint.

Asking everyone where they went to school.

Having a cousin who went to that exact school.

Leaving the footy when the Crows are losing. Ooh, you've got a few of those, haven't you?

Constantly bragging about how good the Barossa is, because it's *heaps good*.

Never letting go of the fact that you were free settlers.

A church.

Another church.

More churches.

And more churches. Yeah, we could be here a while.

The inability to get dinner out after 8:30pm.

A Cibo coffee loyalty card.

A festival pass for all the festivals.

More festival passes for all the festivals.

An overpriced wine tour.

Solar panels.

Driving speeds. Now which one did you want? Because there are only two options: comatose, or maniac.

Saturday night mainies down Hindley Street in your shitbox of a car.

An affinity with Maggie Beer.

Coopers Pale Ale.

The Big Bird costume.

A sighting of a stray cat.

A heap more sightings of a stray cat.

Angle parking in the city.

A tram ticket to Glenelg.

And doing 60km per hour down a four-lane highway.

That's you done, Adelaide. Off you go. Bye!

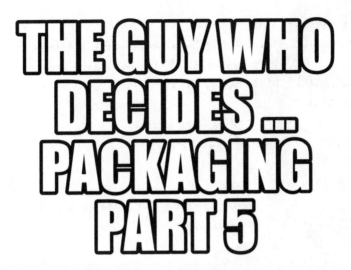

THE GUY WHO DECIDES ... PACKAGING PART 5

Hello, sir, today we're starting with organic fruit and veggies.

> Put a giant plastic sticker on them, Jason.

Do we really need to do that?

> Yes, Jason! How else will they know these things are organic?!

Maybe we could just put them in an organic section, sir?

> Oh, sure, Jason, and then someone might just put some non-organic stuff in the organic section.

But, sir, someone could also just change the stickers around.

> You're right, Jason. Better to be safe than sorry. Wrap 'em in plastic and put a big plastic sticker on 'em. Haha!

But, sir, people who are buying organic stuff don't want plastic—

> YOU HEARD ME, JASON! What's next?

Ah, table salt.

> Put it in a bottle with a twisty lid with some big holes in it and some little holes in it.

Okay. Rock salt?

> A bag.

Okay.

> Wait, Jason! Put some rock salt in a little grinder.

Oh, that's good, sir. So you get some salt *and* a grinder? That's clever.

> Thank you, Jason.

And then to refill your grinder you could just buy the bag of rock salt.

> Pfffffft! No, Jason! You can't refill the grinder! The lid doesn't come off! You idiot!

Right. Um. Self-raising flour?

> Paper bag.

Wholemeal flour?

> Paper bag.

Great, so I'll put cornflour in a paper bag too.

> No, Jason! What are you, an idiot? Cornflour goes in a plastic bag.

Oh, right.

> And then in a box.

Sigh. Umm. Dry spaghetti?

> Plastic bag.

Tortellini?

> Plastic bag.

Rigatoni?

> Plastic bag.

Fettuccine?

> Plastic bag.

Penne?

> Plastic bag.

Lasagne? Plastic bag!

> No, Jason! Lasagne goes in a box!

Sigh. White sugar?

> Paper bag.

Raw sugar?

> Paper bag.

Castor sugar?

> Paper bag

Brown sugar?

> Sluuurrrp.

Sir? You're not saying anything.

> Come on, Jason. See if you can do it. Brown sugar goes in a ...

Um. Paper bag?

> No, Jason! Brown sugar goes in a plastic bag! You get stupider by the millisecond.

AA batteries?

> Lay them down on a piece of cardboard and cover them in plastic. Ha!

Okay.

> And put a little slit in the back so you can press the batteries through the cardboard.

Oh, cool, sir. Easy to open.

> But make it so the batteries never pop out through that cardboard bit, ever.

Right. And watch batteries?

> Put 'em on cardboard and cover them in plastic.

And we'll put that little slit thing in the back again, sir?

> NO!

So, how do they open them?

> You need a pair of scissors and a degree. Haha.

And just remind me of the packaging for scissors again?

> Wrap 'em in the hardest plastic known to humankind. The kind of plastic—

… that you need scissors to open. Yep, got it. Next up, potato chips.

> A plasticky foil bag.

Corn chips?

> Plasticky foil bag.

210

Twisties?

> *Plasticky foil bag.*

Sweet potato chips?

> *Plasticky foil bag.*

Grain Waves?

> *Plasticky foil bag.*

All right. So I'll put Cheezels in—

> *A box!*

What? A box?

> *Yes, Jason. Put them in the foil bag and then put them in a box.*

But isn't that unnecessary?

> *Above your pay grade, Jason.*

Sigh. Fine. Cornflakes?

> *Put them in a bag in a box.*

A ziplock bag, sir? So you can reseal it?

> *No! That's the stupidest idea I ever heard, Jason. Just a sealed bag, which they open, and that's it. And put a little tab and a little hole on the box, that doesn't work properly.*

Right. Bran?

> *In a sealed bag in a box.*

Sultana Bran?

> Sealed bag in a box.

Rice Bubbles?

> Sealed bag in a box.

Weet-Bix?

> You can take this one, Jason.

No sir. I'm not falling for this again.

> Oh, come on, Jason. Give it a go. This is your big chance. All the other cereals were in a sealed bag in a box. What do Weet-Bix go in? Slurrrrrrp.

Umm ... a sealed—

> NO, JASON! Weet-Bix don't go in a sealed bag! They go in an unsealed bag in a box. What are you, an idiot?

Um. Next up. A bar of soap, sir?

> Wrap it in paper.

And—

> And put it in a box.

Banana bread?

> Cut the loaf of banana bread into slices, and then wrap each individual slice in plastic. Ha!

Really?

> And then rearrange the loaf in a cardboard tray. Haha. Slurrrrp. And then wrap it in plastic. Are we done yet, Jason? I'm busy. I've got to decide use-by dates.

Just a couple more, sir. Smartphones?

> Cover every inch of the phone in a plastic film, and then lay it on a little tray. And put it in a coffin.

A coffin, sir?

> You heard me, Jason.

Okay. Last two. Dead people?

> A box.

Murdered people?

> A bag. Now, take my glass, Jason. You can have the last sip. I'm off. Bye!

Oh. Bye, sir. Very kind, sir. *Slurrrp. Splutter.* Whoah, that *is* strong.

THE GUY WHO DECIDES ... ANIMALS

Hello, sir. Another drink, sir?

> Hello, Jason. *Slurrrrrp*. Did you know that my great-great-great-grandfather used to design animals?

Really, sir? What a coincidence. My great-great-great-grandfather used to work for someone who designed animals.

Cue psychedelic travel-back-in time music.

Hello, sir. Your rum toddy, sir. Any last changes to the koala, sir?

> Oh, yes, the koala. Make it eat only toxic leaves, which make it feel really sleepy and kind of drunk. *Slurrrrp*. Hahaha.

I see, sir.

> Ooh, and make its fingerprints indistinguishable from human fingerprints, so that the coppers get koalas confused with felons. Yes. Do that.

Are you sure that's wise, sir?

> Of course I'm sure! Do it.

As you wish, sir. And the giant squid, sir?

> Oh, the giant squid. So big. Make it eat a quarter of a ton of food every day.

Right you are, sir.

> And make its food pass by its brain, so that if it eats anything too big when it swallows it'll give it a brain haemorrhage.

That seems rather unkind, sir.

> You heard me!

I shall make it so, sir. What of the cheetah, sir?

> Make it the fastest animal on Earth. Slurrrrp. But give it horrendous anxiety, so that it's always rather fretful. Haha.

I shall jot that down, sir. And sea snakes?

> Make them unable to drink sea water.

Sir?

> So they spend most of their life dehydrated, trying to find fresh water, in the sea. Ha. Slurrrrp.

Err. I see, sir. And, the panda sir?

> Make them incredibly cute and cuddly so that everyone will want to see them. But then give them no sex drive whatsoever, so that they don't reproduce very often. Haha. Do that.

And mice, sir?

> Make them small and pesty-like, with an uncanny knack for reproducing. So there'll be billions and billions of them.

Should we not switch that around with the pandas, sir?

>*Pffffffft. No, Jason the First. Shut up, Jason the First! You have the mental capacity of a gnat!*

Sorry, sir. Consider me told, sir. What about the ostrich?

>*Make it a massive bird, a huge creature, that can't fly. And make its brain smaller than its eyes. Not unlike yours, Jason the First. Haha.*

Very good, sir. And what of frogs, sir?

>*Frogs are looking pretty good to me, Jason the First.*

Fine, then—

>*Wait! Make it so frogs cannot vomit. But if they really need to vomit, they chuck up their entire stomach. Ha. Approve!*

As you wish, sir. And bats?

>*I like the look of bats thus far. Well done.*

Oh, thank you, sir. So—

>*But! Make them blind.*

Blind, sir? Well, if you say so, sir.

>*And when bats leave a cave, they can only turn left. Like the opposite of Derek Zoolander.*

Who is that, sir?

>*Oh, never mind. I'm having another thought. Give the kangaroos the inability to fart and let's call it a day, eh? Cheers.*

Farewell, sir. *Sigh.* I really need a new vocation.

A GOLD COAST SHOPPING CART

Hi, Gold Coast. I'm your snarky shop assistant for today. Looks like you've got quite a lot there. Who'd have thought? Let's get started, yeah?

Fake tan.

Fake boobs.

Fake nails.

Fake lashes.

Louis Vuitton bag. Sorry, *fake* Louis Vuitton bag.

Hair extensions.

Lash extensions.

Teeth extensions. Weird.

Butt extensions.

Surfboard.

Skateboard.

Rollerblades. No, no. I know it's not Miami. This is definitely the Gold Coast.

An online PT course. Every second person has one of those.

Protein.

Steroids … Don't worry, I won't put that one on the receipt.

An annual theme park pass that you'll only use once.

A bikini. Which you'll wear to the shops with your hair done and in full make-up.

An extra gallon of fake tan.

An abnormally large house.

Laps of the main street in Surfers in your cashed-up bogan car with the fucking personalised plates.

Fireworks at Sea World every night of summer.

Daylight savings. Woops, no. You *don't* want that. Pity. This would have been the perfect place for daylight savings, but whatever.

An eye-roll at the 7000 influencers at the Burleigh Pav.

Gold rings.

Gold chains.

Gold watches.

Gold shoes.

Gold thongs. All to go with your golden glow, right?

Tattoos.

More tattoos.

Oh, a couple more tattoos.

A singlet. Are you going to put that on now? No? You're going to shove it in the back of your shorts. Right.

Forgetting leg day on purpose.

A mild disdain for all the high-rise buildings, even though you live in one. Don't tell me, the only reason you chose to live in a high-rise building was so you'd get the views, but your high-rise building doesn't actually have a view because of another high-rise building blocking your view, and the only view you do have is of your tacky, status-symbol convertible parked in the car park. And by *car park*, I mean the M1.

A night out you can't remember. Oh, looks like you've got a whole bunch of those.

A weekend away at Byron, for a beach holiday.

A caftan or seven

A late-night pitstop at the Macca's at the top of Cavill.

Overpriced spicy margaritas.

Finals tickets to a Gold Coast sporting team. Ha. You won't be needing those.

Fourteen pairs of sunglasses.

A mild hatred of schoolies.

A severe hatred of toolies.

A one-in-four chance you're from New Zealand or the UK.

A subtle underlying aroma of sunscreen and Bondi Sands.

A mole map.

Budgie smugglers.

A visor.

A bum bag.

A friend who has a jetski.

A French bulldog.

A cavoodle in a pram.

A trip to the massage parlour.

A trip down the markets that seem to be on every other day.

The need to drive 20 kilometres below the speed limit.

Dinner, delivered to you on an electric scooter.

An electric scooter.

Sex Wax air freshener.

Sex Wax sticker.

Sex Wax.

Shark repellent so you can swim in the canals.

Someone you know you appeared on *MAFS*.

A sarong.

A toe-ring.

An ankle bracelet.

A blow-up pool.

A Kombi van.

A stubby holder.

A barbecue.

An F45 membership.

Three hours of your life you'll never get back, wandering around Ripley's Believe It or Not.

A slight addiction to leopard print.

And, finally, the inability to do your supermarket shopping after 5pm. And look at that, it's 4:59pm. Just made it. Now get out of here, Gold Coast! Next!

PARENTING FAILS

When you take the kids through the car wash before they're old enough and make them petrified of car washes for life.

When one of your kids poos in the middle of a gathering on a deck.

When you take a photo of your sweetly sleeping kid and the flash comes on and wakes them up.

When you look at your kid's drawing and notice it strangely resembles a dick and balls.

When big brother gives baby brother a haircut.

When your toddler is having nappy-free time and your child-free friends come over. Then the nappy-free kid starts eating his own poo.

When you have to say to your kid, 'You put it *where*?' Because they've put a pom-pom up their nose.

When a drawing from your kid comes home from school and reads: 'My mum likes to sit on the couch and message people all day.'

When you get a fake tan, then the baby feeds and gets an orange face from the fake tan.

When you make a stress ball with a balloon and some flour, and the kid bites the balloon and inhales the flour.

When you give your kid a full-blown inspirational speech, then realise at the end that the kid wasn't even listening.

My mum likes to sit on the couch and message people all day.

BIRDS BE LIKE...

BIRD 1: Hey, man, come over here! Check this out!

BIRD 2: Okay, dude.

BIRD 1: Wow! Wait. What are you doing?

BIRD 2: I'm coming over, like you said.

BIRD 1: But there's a road there.

BIRD 2: Yeah, I know. I'm crossing the road.

BIRD 1: What?!

BIRD 2: Yeah, I'm gonna walk across the road. What's the problem?

BIRD 1: You can't *walk* across the road, mate. There are cars!

BIRD 2: Cars? So?

BIRD 1: So you'll get bloody hit, mate!

BIRD 2: Nah, I'll be right.

BIRD 1: Why would you walk when you can fly?

BIRD 2: Ah, ya gotta flap ya wings and all that to fly. It's easier to walk. It's all good. It's not far.

BIRD 1: Mate, you'll get impaled by a car. Just fly.

BIRD 2: Urgh. Fine then. I'll fly. Here I go.

BIRD 1: Hang on. Why are you facing that way?

BIRD 2: You told me to fly!

BIRD 1: Not that way!

BIRD 2: Huh?

BIRD 1: Well, you can't just fly straight up. You have to take off and get some momentum or you'll get hit by a car!

BIRD 2: Dude, I could have just walked across by now.

BIRD 1: Just turn this way and then fly that way, get over the cars, and then land on the other side!

BIRD 2: So much effort.

BRID 1: It's better than being stuck in a car's front grille, mate!

BIRD 2: You know what? No. I'm not doing all that fancy flying just to get over there. I'll just wait for a break in the traffic and walk across the road.

BIRD 1: Really? Unbelievable.

BIRD 2: Just watch me.
Waiting, waiting. See? Look,
no cars ...

BIRD 1: I really don't want to
watch, mate.

BIRD 2: And now I'm
gonna start my little stroll
across the road.
Easy as.

BIRD 1: Mate! There's a
car coming!

BIRD 2: Dude, it's
miles away.

BIRD 1: Hurry up!

BIRD 2: Dum dee dum ...

BIRD 1: It's getting closer, mate! Just turn around!

BIRD 2: Why would I turn around?

BIRD 1: Because then you'll be out of the way! Mate! Now
there are cars coming from both directions! You're not
going to make it!

BIRD 2: Yes, I am.

BIRD 1: No, you're not! And now you're just standing
there arguing with me! Get off the road!

BIRD 2: Seriously, dude, I know what I'm doing.

BIRD 1: Go back!

BIRD 2: I'm going forward.

BIRD 1: I can't look. I'm closing my eyes.

BIRD 2: Ahhhhhhh ...

BIRD 1: Where'd you go? Did you make it?

BIRD 2: I'm just here. Of course I made it. Now, what were you gonna show me?

BIRD 1: *Phew*. Mate, you almost gave me a heart attack. I was gonna show you this chip packet that still has some crumbs in it.

BIRD 2: You mean that one that's blowing across the road?

BIRD 1: Yeah, that's the one.

BIRD 2: I'll race ya for it.

BIRD 1: You're on!

Beep beep. THUD!

THE GUY WHO DECIDES ... NFTS

Hello, sir. Non-fungible tokens, sir.

NFTs, Jason. Slurrrrrrp.

Sorry, sir. What exactly are they?

I wouldn't expect you to know, Jason. They're a series of letters and numbers that people can buy. But they're not real. They're nothing.

Sorry, what? You're selling nothing?

No, Jason! People are buying a digital thing, like someone's first tweet.

Oh, okay. So, if someone buys that tweet, does that mean it's removed from Twitter?

Nope.

So, everyone can still see it?

Yep.

Really? Well, how much do you pay, then? A dollar?

Pffffffft. No, Jason! 1630 ether.

Annnnd, how much is that?

Oh, about US$3 million, Jason. Slurrrrrp.

What the?! No. Really?

> Really.

Wow. Well, please tell me people can't copy the tweet once it's bought.

> People can still copy it, Jason.

Can they make a screenshot?

> Yes, Jason. But it *is* someone else's.

But why buy it?

> Because those buyers want a bigger dick, Jason!

Right. Of course. What else can you buy?

> Memes from 2011, which everyone's seen a billion times already.

Okay.

> Audio recordings of farts.

Seriously?

> Parts of Logan Paul videos.

Who would want that!?

> A digital fragrance.

Sir, shouldn't people stick to buying things they can actually use in the real world?

> No, Jason!

You don't want to rethink this?

> **Double no, Jason!**

Okay. *Sigh*. So, let me get this straight. You buy a digital item, like an image, that is then your image, and you're the only one who owns that image, but—

> **Jason, Jason, Jason. I'll stop you right there. You don't actually buy the image. What you're really buying is a series of letters and numbers. Or metadata, as people like to call it. And yes, people can still screenshot or share the image that you supposedly bought, all over the internet. Haha!**

But surely if you bought it, you'd own the copyright, sir?

> **Nope.**

What?!

> **The creator owns that, Jason. Ha! Slurrrrrp.**

So the creator can just create the same NFT again?

> **Pffft. What you are, stupid? It's the digital Wild West we're talking about here, Jason. The creator can do whatever the hell they want. If they want to make a thousand more of the things you just bought, they can do that.**

Right. So, say I bought an NFT. Where does it live?

> **On a website, Jason!**

Just a regular, hackable website. Great.

> Or the interplanetary file
> system. Haha. Yeah. Call it
> that.

Right. I feel like I shouldn't ask, but can anyone make an NFT?

> Yes, Jason. Hang on a second.
> That gives me an idea.

No, sir. Please don't, sir. No one will ever buy an NFT of you saying—

> You get stupider by the second, Jason!

Sigh.

> Jason, Jason, Jason.

My god.

> What are you, an idiot?

Are you finished?

> Now, make those into NFTs, Jason!
> Haha! I'm off to the pub.

No one will buy them!

> Shut up, Jason!

THE GUY WHO DECIDES ... COLLECTIVE NOUNS

We have collective nouns today, sir. What do you call a group of guinea pigs?

> A group.

Well. This is going to be fun.

> Ah, good one, Jason. Fun! *Slurrrrrp.* The next one is fun.

Err, the next one was going to be fish.

> That's it then, Jason. A fun of fish.

A fun of fish? Hmmm. It's just that when I think of fish I don't immediately think, 'Oh, let's turn up the music and go *whoop whoop*.'

> Gorillas!

Wait, what?

> A whoop of gorillas, Jason. Write that down.

Oookay. Let's do some birds then. What about geese?

> A flock.

Aha. Parrots?

> A flock!

Seagulls?

> Flock.

Ducks?

> Flock.

Pigeons?

> Flock.

Turkeys?

> Flock.

Are you just going to say flock for everything?

> Slurrrrrrp.

Gawd. What about swifts?

> A flock!

Okay, sir, I can see what's going on here. The next one is crows, so I'll just put a flock of crows and—

> Pffffft. No, Jason! It's a murder of crows! Haha.

Wait, really? A *murder*?

> Shut up, Jason! What's next?

Sheep.

> Let's see ... a flock.

Goats?

> Flock.

Camels?

> Flock.

Well, what about tourists?

> A flock.

Sigh. All right, let's try something different, shall we? Umm. Cats?

> A pounce.

Right. Because they pounce. So, err, creative. Dogs?

> A cry.

Oookay. Tigers?

> An ambush.

Chihuahuas?

> A yap.

Now, that's just silly, sir. *Sigh.* What about this next one, salmon? Should I just put down a *swim* of salmon?

> No, Jason! What are you, an idiot? It's a run of salmon.

Ummm ...

> Slurrrrrrp. Ahhhh.

Because salmon do so much running. Right. So how about guinea fowl?

> A confusion.

Baboons?

> A flange.

Flamingos?

> A flamboyance!

Ravens?

> An unkindness, Jason. No, no, wait! A conspiracy!
> Hahaha.

Sigh. And—

> No, no, no! Make it a *storytelling*! Yeah. Do that.
> Haha. That's a good one. *Slurrrrp.*

Okay, I'll write down *storytelling*.

> No, Jason! Write them all down.

Right. Fine. I'll do that. And how about rooks?

> A storytelling.

So whatever I say next, are you just going to say *storytelling*?

> I don't know, Jason. Will I?

Hawks?

> Hmmm. Hawks. A kettle.

Ah. A kettle?

> Wait! No! A boil! Haha. Do that.

What about foxes?

> A leash.

Deer?

> A leash.

Greyhounds?

> A leash.

Hares?

> Leash.

Rabbits?

> Leash.

Hawks? Oh, wait. We already did that—

> A leash!

Arrrrgh! Hounds?

> A leash!

Right. Leash it is. Now there's just one left. Can we please just have a normal one to finish the day, sir?

> Jason, Jason, Jason. If you would like to be standing where I am standing, then I would estimate that you would have to be 99 per cent less stupid. Now, what's the last one, Jason? Slurrrrrrrp.

Bees.

> Slurrrrrrrrp ... slurrrrrrp .... slurrrrp.

Sir?

> A bike.

What?! A bike?

> Bye, Jason!

Sigh. Yeah, right, because every time I look at some bees, I think, 'Oh, look, there's a bike. Of *bees*.'

> If you're still talking, I'm not listening, Jason! I'm buzzing off, on my bike, Jason! Haha!

Give me strength.

THE GUY WHO DECIDES ... IMPERIAL MEASUREMENTS

Hello, sir. Oops, almost spilled your drink there.

> Hello, Jason. Slurrrrp.

So, today we're deciding how long something is.

> Wonderful, Jason.

Okay. Let's start small, with—

> Line up some barleycorn.

Won't they all be different sizes, sir?

> Do I even have to say it, Jason?

Err, say what, sir?

> Shut up, Jason!

All right, fine. Line up barleycorn. How many?

> Ummm ... three.

Right. Three. And what's that called?

> An inch!

So, three barleycorn is an inch. And if we put some inches together, we should call that something.

> Okay, Jason.

How about a nice round number, like ten?

> Nah, 12.

Really?

> Yes.

Okay. And what do we call that?

> Well, Jason, 12 inches is about the size of my foot. Ha! Slurrrrp.

Yeah, so?

> So, call it a foot, Jason!

A foot! Very good, sir. Very funny. What about a hand?

> A hand? Yes. That's a third of a foot.

Oh. You're serious.

> And a half a hand is called a stick.

Seriously?

> And half a stick is an inch! Hahaha!

Wait. Let me just work that out. So—

> Oh, and, Jason, three of those inches is called a palm. Yeah. Do that.

Aha. Not confusing at all. Sir, can we just go back to the foot. If we put some feet together, what do we get?

> A yard.

Right. So I'll put down that 12 feet is a yard.

> Pffffffft. No, Jason! Why would you say that?!

Well, we had 12 inches in a foot, so I was just keeping with the 12 thing and—

> Jason, Jason, Jason. What experience do you have creating measurement units?

About the same as you, sir. None.

> Pardon, Jason?

Nothing, sir. Go on.

> There will be *three* feet in a yard. Haha.

Fine. What's next?

> A mile.

Sigh. And high many yards in a mile?

> One thousand ...

Oh, well, that's a nice round number.

> ... seven hundred and fifty. Haha! No, wait. Make it sixty.

Soooo, 1760 yards in a mile?

> Yes, Jason. And one-eighth of a mile is a furlong. Haha! Slurrrrp.

Sir, can we just divide stuff by ten, or 100? Just to make it a little simpler?

> Okay, smartypants. We'll divide a furlong by ten.

Oh, you're listening to me? Wow. Okay, sir. And what's that called?

A Gunter's chain!

That's weird. But whatever. What's next?

A fathom!

Okay, so we divide the chain by ten to get a fathom?

Yes.

Great!

Actually, no.

What?

Eleven. Divide it by 11.

Noooo. Sir—

But don't worry, Jason. One hundred fathoms is a cable! Haha!

One hundred?

Yes! You wanted it easier, didn't you, Jason?

It's a bit too late for that.

Oh, and ten cables is a mile.

Wait, wait. That's not right. That maths doesn't work out.

Fine. Call it a nautical mile. Ha!

What? What's a nautical mile?

And three of those is a league.

Wait, just stop. How many feet in a nautical mile?

> Hmmm ... let's say 6000 ... and carry the 1 ... 80.
> Yeah, 6080.

Sorry, sir, but we started at a barleycorn and we've gone to feet and inches and miles and nautical miles, and it's very confusing. Surely it can't all come back around and end up at a barleycorn.

> Say it with me: Jason, Jason, Jason. The school
> that you went to should be ashamed of itself, for
> producing an idiot like you. Slurrrrrp. So, 63,360
> inches equals a standard mile, Jason. Which is not to
> be confused with the Roman mile, which is 60,000
> inches. And while we're speaking of inches, inches
> can be divided by six, and that makes a beaker. And
> guess what, Jason? Twelve points make up a beaker.
> And if you divide a point by six, you get a line, and
> a line is the exact same length ... as a poppyseed.
> And guess what four poppyseeds equals, Jason.

I don't know, a—

> A barleycorn, Jason! Now if you'll excuse me, I'm
> going to fill up my drink somewhere away from you.
> Goodbye, Jason.

Yeah, all right. Bye! That all sounds completely ridiculous. What sort of stupid country would ever use any of that?

THE TODDLER: A REVIEW

Hi, so I thought I should review the toddler for anyone out there who's thinking of getting one. Mine is the early 2019 model, with the blonde hair and blue eyes. I've had it for a few years now, got it brand new, and I'm generally pretty happy with it. It's definitely cute, most of the time, and in great condition. But I read on some forums that people are experiencing a few issues with theirs, like tantrums and stuff. I have had a little of that, but things are generally okay if I keep the food and sleep levels steady. I did find a hack that might be worth trying – when the toddler is starting to get a little feral, a bribe can work, like a small piece of chocolate or a shiny new Hot Wheels car. Overall, I am super happy with my toddler and would recommend it. It can get a bit stinky at times, but that's usually an easy fix. Keep in mind you do have to maintain your toddler, and it will cost you a bit of money. If you're thinking of getting one, be on the lookout for some deals. In our case we got two for the price of one. They look almost the same, and they have been amazing. Highly recommend. If I was to think of any downsides it would be the bags under my eyes, which are due to the early start-up time of these models. They do like to go flat out all day, and their batteries are ridiculous. Hope that helps!

A CANBERRA SHOPPING CART

Oh, hi there, Canberra. Shopping all done? Great. It's time to see you what your essential items are. Shall we?

Lanyards. Of course.

Roundabouts. So many roundabouts. I don't know how you don't get dizzy.

Constantly defending Canberra, saying it's not boring, when you actually realise it is boring because the main event for the year is an international flower show called Floriaaaaaade.

Getting some great deals from *The COC*, on Iron Knob Street.

Spotting politicians in public and not giving a shit. Oh, you're buying those in bulk, I see.

Going to a wedding at Old Parliament House. Another bulk purchase, of course.

A bomb shelter that doubles as bus stop. Or is it the other way round? Hard to know.

Flexing about the fact that you're the number one city in the world at Wordle. Whoop-de-do.

A school trip to Questacon. What's that? You can never have too many of those? Whatever you say.

Constantly telling people that Canberra has other attractions aside from adult movies and fireworks.

A statue of a penis. What do you mean it's *not* a penis? An owl? Right. You tell yourself that.

Always being annoyingly freezing. Not freezing enough to have snow, though, which would at least be a fun kind of cold.

A cancelled Qantas flight. Or several. Yep, definitely several.

A hail warning. Another hail warning. And another. We'll get more in tomorrow, don't worry.

A trip down to 'Bato' to escape the people who live in your suburb, but when you get there everyone from your suburb is there.

Four out of five people are public servants.

And the remaining person is a cyclist in Lycra.

Bike lanes on every single road, except for where cyclists actually want to cycle.

An electric scooter.

Getting used to the fact that when you tell someone from overseas that you're from Canberra, they say, 'Where's that?'

Getting annoyed that the news says 'Canberra made this decision' and 'Canberra did that' when it's actually the politicians who live in Canberra who made those decisions, *and* that those politicians don't really even live in Canberra, they just fly in and out of Canberra.

Driving past a farm or two on your way to work.

A walk around the lake in the direction of your choosing.

A Kathmandu puffer jacket. Or three. Yeah, they'll go nicely with your hail warnings.

A large groan if ever you have to drive more than 20 minutes.

Posting a pic on Insta of the view from Mount Taylor.

Being annoyed that you're stuck in rush hour, which lasts for ten minutes.

A random encounter with a rogue emu.

Almost hitting a kangaroo.

Hot-air balloon tickets, which you haven't used because of the fog.

Lots of hot air because of the hot-air balloons, and the politicians.

The inability to drive at 100 kilometres an hour, by law, on a road.

Getting loose at 'The Moose'.

A hangover from getting loose at 'The Moose'.

A trip to Kingsley's Chicken shop, because you're hungover from getting loose at 'The Moose'.

Lane one form.

Signs that say 'Lane one form', when the rest of Australia says 'Form one lane'.

Never surrendering when merging. Sorry, I meant when *lane one forming*.

The unwritten rule that the heater doesn't go on till after Anzac Day.

This gesture. *Clap*. Did I do that right? Clapping my hands above my head? It has something to do with Vikings, yeah?

Being the most vaccinated city in the world. First jab, second jab, third jab, fourth etc.

Being from the north and not wanting to go south.

Being from the south and not wanting to go north.

Bogans, bogans and more bogans.

Burnouts, burnouts and more burnouts.

Bogans *and* burnouts. Sorry, I should say *Summernats*.

Talking about your APS level. Yeah, you will need *a lot* of those.

An APS 6 telling you about their EL1 secondment.

Overpriced rentals.

When talking to someone from Queanbeyan, constantly making the joke about needing to see their passport. Never gets old, right?

Referring to the city as *Civic*.

Overpriced parking in Civic.

Getting a parking fine in Civic.

Fleece-lined activewear.

Nothing being open in January.

Realising for the first time, right now, that you've been saying *Mah*-nukka for all these years, when it's actually Ma-*noo*-ka.

Protestors. Heaps and heaps of protestors.

Being annoyed at all those protestors, regardless of whether you think they're right or wrong.

Weed. *Cough.* By which I mean a common weed from your garden, of course, right? *Wink.*

And finally, lime milk. Whatever that is.

Okay, that's you done, Canberra. Oh, and that *will* be 20 per cent more than anywhere else because, well, you live in Canberra. Next!

THE GUY WHO DECIDES ... OLYMPIC SPORTS PART 2

Hello, sir, some more decisions to make about Olympic events today.

> Ah yes, Jason.

Remember, we're talking the pinnacle of human sporting ability here.

> Horse jumping.

No, no. We already did that one, sir. Peak *human* performance.

> Walking.

Err. Walking?

> Yep!

Sorry, just to clarify, sir. Walking?

> Yes, Jason! Walking, but make it a race.

Wouldn't that be running?

> Jason, Jason, Jason. Sometimes a race isn't about how fast you can go. Sometimes, it's about how fast you can go with one heel always on the ground. Haha! Slurrrrrp.

250

Right. Walking. What else?

> Boat racing.

Okay. What kind of boat?

> A sailboat. Ooh, and *backwards* boat racing. Hehe.

Sorry?

> People row a boat and when they cross the finish line, they'll be backwards.

Right. And how do they steer?

> With their cox. Slurrrrrp.

With their *cocks*, sir!? But—

> You heard me, Jason!

Err. So, how do the women steer?

> Jason, Jason, Jason. The men and the women both have cox.

Um …

> It's a coxswain, Jason! Get your mind out of the gutter. It's the lightweight person who sits in the boat and steers.

And are they facing backwards, too?

> Pfffft. No, Jason! What are you, an imbecile? They're facing the right way.

All right. So there's four people rowing, and the cox—

> No, Jason! Four people don't need a coxswain!

Well, how do *they* steer?

> They don't.

So, they're facing the right way, then?

> Nope.

I give up. What else have you got?

> Swimming!

Okay, great. So, the fastest person from one end of the pool to the other?

> Yep. We'll call that freestyle.

Oh, are there other styles?

> Yeah, why not? How about facing-the-roof swimming?

Facing-the-roof swimming? Err, so—

> And butterfly!

But, sir, butterflies aren't really known for their swimming ability—

> Shut up, Jason! Titty stroke.

What!? No, no, sir. You can't call a style that.

> Boob stroke, then.

No, sir.

> Melons stroke.

Uh uh.

> Bosom stroke.

No!

> Double D—

No, no, no, sir. *Sigh.* We could probably get away with, um, breast ... stroke? Let's just go with that, okay?

> Urgh. Fine.

I think that's swimming done, sir.

> Ooh, here's one. Fencing!

Oookay.

> Yes! Let the competitors put up the fences for the horses in the sandpit, so they can jump over them. Hahaha. Slurrrrp.

Err.

> And they can put up the fences as fast they can for the 110-metre jumpy-over-fency race! And for the steeplechase!

The steeplechase, sir?

> Yeah! That can be where people run around pretending to be horses, Jason. And they can jump over horse fences, and over a little pond! Haha!

That sounds very silly. Sir, what if fencing was actually—

> Ooh, I've got another one! Sword fighting!

Yeah, that's—

> Shut up, Jason! Flexible, bendy, not-so-sharp sword pokey-pokey fighting. Yeah!

Umm. I'll just write that one down then. Bendy, bendy—

> Handball!

Sir?

> Throw a little ball into a little soccer goal! Ha!

Oh, okay. That could work.

> Ooh, and handball, but in a swimming pool!

Really? Like, in a shallow pool?

> *Nope.*

Then how do they keep themselves above the water if they have to throw a ball?

> *With their hands, Jason.*

Sir, they can't just grip the water.

> *They use the squirrel grip. Hahaha. Slurrrrp.*

Sigh.

> *Ooh, and how about this one? Roly-poly. Wait! No! Greco-Roman roly-poly. Yeah. Do that.*

Sir, what on Earth would that—

> *Volleyball!*

Oh, okay. That one sounds promising.

> *And! Bikini volleyball!*

Oh, god. Sir, there's absolutely no reason for *that*.

> *Fine! Then put it on the beach! Ha!*

So, on sand?

> *Yeah! Oh, and I've got another one! Top Gun volleyball!*

No! Sir! That's going too far.

> *Bouncy bouncy.*

Sir, are you talking about bikini volleyball again?

> *No, Jason! Different sport. Its full name is bouncy bouncy flippy flippy.*

Umm ...

> They bounce on a trampoline, Jason!

Right. What else?

> Riding a bike.

That's it?

> Riding a bike on a road. And also riding a bike in a Beyblade stadium—

Sir—

> And riding your kid's bike. Over little hills. And riding through some trees.

Wow. That's a lot of riding.

> Ooh! And riding around a Beyblade stadium, in a line.

Sir, I think that's—

> And doing sick flips on your kid's bike. Ha!

Sigh. Right.

> And playing cat and mouse, on a bike, in a Beyblade stadium.

That's enough of the bikes, sir.

> I've got more!

Shut up, sir!

> What did you just say, Jason?

Umm, nothing, sir. I said nothing.

> Slurrrrp.

Um. Should I go, sir?

> No, Jason. You will stay. And, because you think
> you're so smart, you can make up an Olympic sport,
> Jason. Go on. Your turn.

Umm ... errr ...

> I'm waiting.

Um. Boxing?

> What!?

Sorry. I meant punchy punchy in the facey facey.

> Mmm. Go on.

In a ... ring?

> A ring? Hmm. And?

Oh, you want more? Um. In a ring, and ... I dunno, sir. I've run out of—

> Jason, Jason, Jason. This just proves that you are
> even more stupid than I thought.

Sorry, sir. What would you add to punchy punchy in the facey facey?

> Easy. Pillows on their hands, Jason!

Right. Why didn't I think of that?

> And make the ring square. Ha!

A *square* ring, sir? Isn't that—

> Are we done, Jason?

Umm .... no?

> Shut up, Jason. We're done.

THE GUY WHO DECIDES ... WORDLE

Morning, sir. How about a new game, sir?

> You look different, Jason. Slurrrrp.

New glasses, sir.

> You look like an idiot.

Right. Anyway, back to the new game. So—

> A word game!

Okay, great.

> Guess the five-letter word, Jason.

Okay.

> Sluuurrrp.

Oh, is that it? There aren't any clues?

> It's a five-letter word, Jason. What more do you need?

That's not really a clue, sir.

You get six chances.

Okay, sir. But we probably need to have a bit more to it.

We'll tell them if they guess a correct letter.

How?

With a yellow square.

Okay, great. So a correct letter in the correct place gets a yellow—

Pffffft. No, Jason! That's a green square!

Oh, so you get to figure out the word from the colour of the squares from your previous guesses?

Yeah!

And if you solve the puzzle, you get another one!

Pfffft. No, Jason!

What? So, that's it? Just one word?

Every 24 hours. Hahaha!

Really, that's seems stupid.

You're stupid, Jason.

Sigh. So, to play this game you download the app from the app store.

Nope.

Umm ... you download the app from a website?

Nup.

Ah! It's a physical game, with little tiles and—

No!

You play it on Nintendo?

> Nah.

PlayStation?

> No.

Xbox?

> No, Jason! You just play it on the website.

Right. But you can only play it once a day?

> Yep. It remembers. Ha! Slurrrrrrp.

Oookay. And what's this game called?

> Word—hiccup—ull.

Pardon?

> Word—hiccup—ull.

Sorry, are you saying *Wordle*?

> Sure. That'll do.

Right. So, to play, you go to wordle.com—

> Pffffft. No, Jason!

What? Why not?

> You go to nytimes.com/games/wordle.

Umm, sir—

> Shut up, Jason!

Sigh. Okay.

> Moist.

Sorry?

> What are you, an idiot? People's first five-letter guess will be moist.

Right.

> Or crane.

Okay. I get it. People's first guess will be a word with vowels in it, and common letters.

> Yes, Jason! And then after a few goes, people will start trying to make up random words with the leftover letters. Ha!

Right. Anything else?

> Yeah. It's the same word for everyone in the whole world.

Oh, but, sir. What about spoilers?

> Yeah!

So, one person could ruin it for everyone?

> Yep! And people will hate other people for that! Hahaha. Slurrrrrp.

Oookay.

What's with that tone, Jason?

Well, sir, I just think it's a bit, um, basic.

Jason, Jason, Jason. it's funny you should use the word basic. Because that's what you're in my phone as. Basic McBasic-Face.

Sigh.

Wordle will go viral. Haha! And every boring loser who sits at a desk all day will play it, so they have something to talk to Jennifer from accounts about.

That's a bit rude, sir.

Shut up, Jason. Actually, you'd get along with Jennifer. I should set you two up on a date. Haha.

No, no. No need, sir. So, what's the Wordle word for today?

Slurrrrrp. Hmmm … penis.

Right.

Goodbye, Jason! I'm going to the bar. And I'll have a word to Jennifer!

261

THE GUY WHO DECIDES ... NETFLIX

Hello, sir.

> Jason, put all the TV on the internet.

Um. Okay.

> And then people can watch it whenever, wherever.

Sounds good. So, what's on there?

> Tens of things.

Tens of things?

> No, wait! Make it hundreds of things.

Err ...

> No! Thousands! No! Tens of thousands of things!
> Yeah. Slurrrrp.

Wow. That's a lot of things, sir. Do you think—

> Yep!

And do people pay for this?

> Yes, Jason! About $10 a month.

Oh, well, that's pretty good. Heaps of TV and movies in HD—
    Pffffffft. No, Jason! SD, not HD!

Right, so what does HD cost then?
    About $15 a month.

Okay, but what you're telling me is that, either way, people
will have something to watch every single night. That's—
    No, Jason! People will have so
    much choice that they won't
    know what to watch. Ha!

Ah, sorry?
    You heard me, Jason!
    There'll be so many things
    to watch that people won't watch anything. Hehe.

Well, let's take some of the choice away, sir.
    Shut up, Jason! No. We'll give them even more choice.
    By adding foreign movies. And foreign TV.

But they'll be in a separate category, right?
    Nope.

Subtitles?
    Dubbed!

But how will they tell if it's a foreign TV show or movie?
    Jason, Jason, Jason. They're going to have to
    watch the first five minutes. You know, the part
    where nothing really happens. And then, after five
    minutes, when the first person in the movie or TV
    show actually speaks, the people watching will finally
    realise it's dubbed. Haha!

That's just mean, sir. Do people *ever* find anything to watch?

> Yes, Jason!

Oh, phew. So is it, like, every Wednesday there's a new episode? So people know what to expect?

> Pffffft. No, Jason! What are you, an idiot? We'll just put the whole series up at once. And make each episode just roll on into the next.

Oookay. So, like, after the credits—

> Credits? No, Jason. No one wants credits.

But they're important, sir.

> All right, fine! You can have five seconds of credits. Then onto the next episode!

Well, that's hardly enough time to find out who the key grip was.

> Shut up, Jason!

What happens when people *do* find something to watch?

> They stay up all night, Jason.

What?!

> You heard me, Jason. And then in the morning when they arrive at work, they're really cranky. Slurrrrrp.

So, it takes forever to find something, and then once you do, you can't stop?

> Yep! Ha!

Right. And what else?

> Trending.

264

Trending?

> Yes, Jason! Put trending shows on the main page.

Oh, like a brand new TV show or the latest—

> No, Jason! Make it a kids' movie, and a TV series from the '90s. And a foreign film. Not that anyone would know until they've watched it for five minutes. Ha! Oh, and throw in a bad comedy and an even worse action-adventure film that flopped at the box office in 2017. Haha. Yeah. Do that.

I don't even know what to say. Ah …

> Oooh, and Jason! When the people turn it on, they get a fright.

I don't understand, sir. Are you saying that when they sit down to watch, they get—

> BA BoooooMMMM!

Arrgh! Oh. Whoa.

> Hahahaha. Slurrrrp.

Right. Well, despite all that, and the fright at the start, I think it's going to be a good service, sir. Heaps of film and TV, all in one place for—

> No, Jason! There'll be other streaming services just like this one.

Hahaha. Very good, sir. You almost got me there.

> Slurrrrrp.

Oh, you're serious, sir. So, people *really* won't be able to find anything to watch. Can I ask how many other ones there are?

Disney +, Apple TV+, Binge, Foxtel, Kayo, Stan ...

Oh, god.

Hulu, Hayu, BritBox, Amazon—

Okay, enough. And how much do those ones cost?

About $15 a month. Each. Bye, Jason!

Bye, sir. Great. So, people have gone from
paying absolutely nothing for free-to-air TV to
paying a crapload for all these subscriptions
to watch absolutely nothing. Good one, sir.
Awesome.

BA BOOOOOMMMM!

A PERTH
SHOPPING CART

Oh, hi there, Perth. I'll be your judgey shop assistant for today. Let's see what you've got ...

Brunch at a chic-looking cafe with hideous coffee.

Plane tickets from 2020 that you still haven't used.

A year's worth of wine that you bought down in Margaret River.

Drinking said wine in one weekend.

Swimming with dolphins.

Swimming with sharks.

Swimming with whales.

Swimming with whale sharks.

Swimming with seals.

Swimming with penguins.

Whatever else you can swim with, you're going to swim with it.

A selfie with a quokka.

A holiday to Bali for the weekend.

Bragging to the people over east that you've holidayed in Bali for the weekend.

A friend having a beach wedding in Bali.

A time-share apartment in Bali.

Seventeen hats.

A gallon of 50+ sunscreen, even though you think you should have 500+ sunscreen.

Tickets to Optus Stadium to see the Eagles and Freo.

Sweating all day waiting for your knight in shining armour, the Freo Doctor.

Everything closed at 5pm on a Monday. And a Tuesday. And a Wednesday etc.

Every fourth person is from New Zealand.

Every third person is from Ireland.

Every second person is from South Africa.

A trip to a brewery.

Crappy internet speeds. Probably because it has to come from over east.

A closed border. Wow, you've really stocked up on those, haven't you?

An evening watching the sun set and taking a pic. And putting it on Insta because if it didn't go on Insta it never happened. And the reason you put it on Insta in the first place is because you're flexing at the people over east that Perth is actually the sunniest capital city in the world, but because you're two or three hours behind, and due to the crappy internet speeds, those people over east will be in bed by the time the pic goes up, and so they won't actually see it.

At least 10,000 photos of a black swan.

Mentioning that Hugh Jackman went to WAAPA.

A romantic rendezvous in Kings Park.

Reminding people that Heath Ledger was from Perth.

A holiday house in the south-west.

A caravan, because you *don't* have a holiday house in the south-west.

A G2G form or two. Or more like 700.

Approximately 200 varieties of craft beer, but only craft beer that's been made in WA.

A strong intuition about whether someone is from *the other side of the river*.

Being told by people from over east that you have 'a slight accent', and you're like, 'Yeah, nah.'

The genuine problem that you can't figure out which beach to go to.

Havaianas.

Budgie smugglers.

About 700 bajillion square kilometres of land, but everyone's squashed into near Perth.

Thinking that everyone in this city can't drive. Hmmm ... perhaps that includes you.

Using the word *FIFO* in every conversation. Yeah, better grab a few more of those.

Hayfever tablets.

A run along the beach.

Activewear you don't get active in.

Taking pictures and laughing at trucks stuck under the

Bayswater Bridge.

A small hole in your head from a magpie. Yes, those *are* cheaper by the dozen.

Peter Alexander pyjamas.

An inferiority complex.

A long mac, *topped up*.

The want to ask everyone where they grew up.

Saying 'it's a dry heat'. Yep, just grab the whole box of those. May as well.

A snorkel.

A shemozzle of a TV schedule.

Calling the toilet a *thunder box*.

Always seeing someone you know when you go out, especially when you're in Bali.

Not caring that this is the only place in the world where you call your premier 'State Daddy'.

And, of course, waiting two weeks for a delivery because everything comes from over east.

Okay, are we done? We're done. See ya, Perth. Next!

A DARWIN SHOPPING CART

So how are we, Darwin? How's your day been? Sticky? No kidding. Anyways, I'm here to check out your shopping and see what it says about you. Let's get started ...

Beers.

Beers.

Beers.

A mate with a boat.

A trip to the Mindil markets.

Crocodiles.

Crocodiles.

Crocodiles.

Jellyfish. Yeah, I've lost count of those.

Watching an amazing sunset every single night.

Never going in the water at the amazing sunset every

night because of all the crocodiles and jellyfish, even though you really want to go in the water because Darwin is, like, the hottest place on Earth, and going in the water would be the logical thing to do, if it wasn't for all the crocodiles and jellyfish.

Two thousand per cent humidity.

A dehumidifier. But really, what's the point?

Having a shower every hour because of the humidity.

Needing a shower while you're *in* the shower because of the humidity.

Mould, because of the humidity.

Having the fan running all year round to try to get rid of the dampness.

Going fishing.

Hoping to catch a million-dollar fish when you're going fishing.

Getting around town in your fishing shirt.

'CU in the NT' merch.

Even though it's stinking hot and you'd think it was the last thing anyone would want to eat ... a laksa. For breakfast, at Mary's.

A four-wheel drive with super-high suspension.

Hunting lights for your four-wheel drive.

A knife.

A gun.

A mullet.

Copious amounts of YETI merch.

Knowing what 'the Berrimah Line' is.

Blaming Canberra for everything. Times 100 or so, yeah?

Referring to the rest of Australia as 'down south'.

Rolling your eyes at the blow-ins from 'down south'.

Checking the BOM app every three seconds in the wet season, hoping that it says it's going to be dry, even though you just know it's going to be wet.

Mowing the lawn in your jocks. I can't unsee *that*.

Putting on the only jumper you own when the temperature dips below 25 degrees.

Fangin' it down Dick Ward Drive to Fannie Bay.

Speed limits. Nah.

Road rules. Who needs them, right?

A heater. Nah to that too.

Croc burgers.

Barramundi burgers.

Anything-you-can-kill burgers.

Crocodiles. Oh, did we already do those? Whatever. *More* crocodiles.

A Bintang singlet from Bali, *not* worn ironically.

A pool.

Four different types of esky – the good one, the one for going out, the one for in the car and the motorised esky.

The phrase, 'Just wait for dry season.' Yeah, grab a whole box of those.

Waiting for dry season.

Feeding the fish.

A school trip to Singapore.

Beers, beers, beers … at Monsoons.

More beers, at a place called Shenannigans.

Not catching the million-dollar fish.

Living in the only place in the world where the leader is growing a mullet.

Shoes ... are optional.

Waterfalls that are better than Queensland's waterfalls.

A photo at said better-than-Queensland waterfall.

A stop-off at the Humpty Doo.

Walking around at an extremely slow pace so as to not break into a sweat.

A random party on a sandbar.

Those orange e-scooters.

Using a fishing or hunting profile pic on Tinder.

Someone swiping right on your fishing or hunting profile pic on Tinder. Actually, scrap that.

High-vis anything.

LandCrusiers.

Fireworks for Territory Day.

Not knowing how to use the fireworks on Territory Day.

And last one ... thinking you're tougher than the rest of Australia because you live in the NT. That is *so* you, Darwin. Next!

GOING TO SLEEP BE LIKE...

BRAIN: Well, that was a big day.

LEGS: Tell me about it. I was out in the sun all day!

BRAIN: All right, pipe down. Everyone, it's time to chill out. We're going to sleep, okay?

EYES: Whoa! The light! I can't stop looking at it, dude.

BRAIN: Yeah, TikTok *is* pretty awesome, eh? Hehe. Wait. No, stop! What are we doing? It's sleep time. Arms! Put the phone away!

ARMS: Whatever you say, man.

BRAIN: All right. System check. Legs, how are you doing down there? Feeling relaxed?

LEGS: Yeah, mate. I'm pretty good.

BRAIN: Arms?

ARMS: Yep, I'm doing okay, man.

BRAIN: How about you, Torso?

TORSO: Oh, this blanket is amazing. I'm so warm, thanks.

FEET: I'm f-f-f-freezing!

BRAIN: But you've got socks on!

FEET: And they're doing jack shit!

BRAIN: Urgh. Always complaining.

EYES: So many colours, dude.

BRAIN: Eyes! Close yourselves! We're meant to be getting ready for sleep!

EYES: Sorry, dude.

BRAIN: Righto. That's better. Everyone seems relaxed.

STOMACH: *Arrrgh. Grumble. Gurrrrgle.*

BRAIN: What the—

STOMACH: *Burrrrrrrrrp.* That's better.

BRAIN: Shut up, Stomach!

STOMACH: Don't tell me what to do. *Burrrrrrrrp.*

BRAIN: Eyes!? Closed!

EYES: Oh yeah, sorry, dude.

BRAIN: Can everyone please just chill out?
Slow transition to sleep mode, okay?
Pineal Gland, we need some melatonin.

PINEAL GLAND: You know what? *No.*
I'm not talking to you.

BRAIN: Oh, god. Not this again. Hey, Suprachiasmatic
Nucleus, you're the only one she'll talk to.

SUPRACHIASMATIC NUCLEUS: Urgh. Always got to
do your dirty work. Yoohoo, Pineal Gland? Could we
have a little melatonin please?

PINEAL GLAND: Ooh, you're so hot and
suprachiasmatic. Anything for you, darling. But I will
need absolute silence, okay?

BRAIN: *Sigh.* Everyone, shut up!

PINEAL GLAND: All right. Here comes the melatonin.
Hmmmmm. Ahhhhhh ...

BRAIN: Are you done?

PINEAL GLAND: Di-di-di. No interruptions.

BRAIN: Urgh. Every damn night.

RANDOM THOUGHT: Hey! Hi!

BRAIN: Who are you?

RANDOM THOUGHT: Don't mind me. I'm just a
random thought. Hey, it's great here.

BRAIN: Get out!

PINEAL GLAND: Shhhhh! You're interrupting my rhythm. Ommmmm.

ANOTHER RANDOM THOUGHT: Boo! Hahaha!

BRAIN: What the hell? Who are *you*?

ANOTHER RANDOM THOUGHT: Just another random thought. But you can call me Art.

BRAIN: Argh. Tonight is not the night, guys. Both of you, out!

RANDOM THOUGHT: Killjoy.

ANOTHER RANDOM THOUGHT: Yeah, you're no fun.

BRAIN: Right. That's better. Where were we?

PINEAL GLAND: Mmmmmelatonin. Go, my pretties. Go, go!

BRAIN: Ahhhh .... Nice one. Looks like we're back on track.

STRESSFUL THOUGHT: Oi! Did you send that invoice?!

BRAIN: Please, no.

ADRENAL GLANDS: Did someone say stress?! Release the hounds!

STRESS HORMONES: Rarrrrrrgh! Arrrrgh! Garrrrrrrr!

EYES: Whoa, dude ...

PINEAL GLAND: Oh, good one, Brain!

BRAIN: It wasn't *me*!

ADRENAL GLANDS: More! More! More!

BRAIN: Stop it, Adrenal Glands! It's just a damn email! We'll send it in the morning!

ADRENAL GLANDS: Oh. It's just an email? Okay.

EYES: That was gnarly, dude.

PINEAL GLAND: Goodness, what a carry-on.

BRAIN: Stress gone? Good. Peace at last.

LEGS: I'm hot!

BRAIN: Urgh. Well, take the blanket off.

LEGS: Okay. Oh. Now I'm cold!

BRAIN: Just put one leg out!

LEGS: Oh, that's better, thanks.

BRAIN: Begin muscle paralysis procedure.

ARMS: Ahhhhhh ...

LEGS: Ahhhhh ...

EYES: Duuuuuude ...

FEET: Sh-sh-sh-shiver ...

THAT RANDOM JERK: Yo! What's up?

BRAIN: No! *Not* tonight!

THAT RANDOM JERK: Rah! Hahaha.

BRAIN: Stop it, please.

THAT RANDOM JERK: Booooo! Hehehe.

BRAIN: Please. Don't wake everyone up. We only just—

THAT RANDOM JERK: Just messing with you, dude. I'll go.

BRAIN: Really? Thank you.

THAT RANDOM JERK: RRRAAAAAARRRR!

BRAIN: Nooooo!

ARMS: Hnnn ...

LEGS: Shhh ....

EYES: F-f-lutter.

FEET: B-b-b-r-r.

TORSO: Wh-wh-wh ...

BUTTHOLE: *Parrrrp.*

BRAIN: Phew. Somehow, everyone stayed asleep. We're almost there.

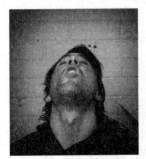

BLADDER: Nnnnnnng.

BRAIN: What are you doing, Bladder?

BLADDER: *Garrrrrrgle.*

BRAIN: Please, no. We're almost asleep.

BLADDER: *Garrrr-rrrr-rrrgle.*

BRAIN: NOOOO!

LEGS: Wake up! We're going to the toilet!

ARMS: The toilet?! Righto!

FEET: Awwww, I *just* got warm!

EYES: Whoa, what's going on?!

BRAIN: *Sigh.* Why do I even bother?

MEANWHILE AT A BUNNINGS SAUSAGE SIZZLE ...

... only this sausage sizzle is run by the ladies from Briiiiiighton.

Sausages! Get your posh sausages, darlings!

Yes, try our mushroom and summer truffle mustard, darlings!

TRADIE: Um ... just a normal snag and bread for me, thanks.

No, no, sir, you don't want that. You want the sausage with Porsche cayenne and cinnamon relish.

TRADIE: Nah, just tomato sauce, thanks.

Oh, darling, they all want tomato sauce!

Oh, darling, that's because there's no culture here in
Mooooooorabbin.

Mmm. More like Moooo-rabid dogs, darling.

TRADIE: G'day, ladies, just a snag with onions, ta.

Pardon?

Darling, what's he saying?

I don't know.

Sorry, we don't know what you're saying. But here's a wanker sausage for you, on sourdough with almond pâté.

TRADIE: Oh, right. I've got some gold coins here for you ...

Some what?! Oh, no, we don't do cash. Platinum, if you don't mind.

TRADIE: No worries, I can use my card. Here you go. Whoa. What the hell!? That's one expensive snag!

Yes, that's because it's for the poor people.

More sourdough, Nancy!

Of course, darling. And more sausages too. Italian Casalinga ...

Lamb Sangiovese with caramalised apple?

Pork, white chocolate and duck?

Ruinarrrrrrt and rabbit?

Pecorino, plum and Platinum?

Beef, Bobo and lime?

Fennel and Pfiiiiiiizer?

Ooh, and how are the beef, gooseneck and barnacle sausages coming along, Margo? Margo?

Oh, don't poke the bear, darling. Margo's in a mooooood.

She is? Why, darling?

You mean you don't know what happened at her 65th?

Do tell, darling.

Poor Jane ran out of Ruinarrrrrrt.

No way.

Way, darling. Margo had to move to Prahran.

RANDOM BLOKE: Well, this is a bit fancy, ladies.

Oh, hello, handsome. And yes, we are, darling.

And we don't look a day over 44, darling.

Just a single sausage, sir, or are you in a relationship?

RANDOM BLOKE: Err ...

Get this lovely man a Briiiiiighton special, Nancy!

With pleasure, darling. There you go.
Num num.

Ooh, look. Elvira is finally here.

Ah, yes, late as always.

Oh, but look at her. Is that fresh Bobo?

It is, darling. She looks marvellous. You
wouldn't know she was so sad.

Well, of course not, darling.
That's because she can't move
her face. But why is she sad,
darling?

Didn't you hear? Her Michael has been banging the
female chimney sweep again.

A chimney sweep?!

Yes, darling. You sound shocked, darling. Do you not have a chimney sweep? I have my chimney swept three times a week.

But, darling, you don't even have a chimney.

ANOTHER RANDOM: Excuse me, could I just have a—

Nancy! Get this man a gooseneck barnacle!

ANOTHER RANDOM: Oh, I see your sign says you're raising money for poor people. Good on you, ladies. Who—

Yes, it's for the poor people of the yacht club. They need money for the underground aquarium car park, don't you know?

ANOTHER RANDOM: The ... what?

There's your sausage. That'll be $37.50. On Platinum?

ANOTHER RANDOM: What?! This is—

Grab the Ruinarrrrrt, darling! Time to go! The natives are getting restless!

A HOBART SHOPPING CART

Shut up, Hobart! Oops, I mean, hello, Hobart! Let's see what very Tassie items you've got for yourself today ...

Hitting up the Salamanca Market, but only if you can get a park out the front and if you can't, forget it.

Being quite progressive.

Complaining about being quite progressive.

A trip to the mainland.

Bringing home a box of Krispy Kremes from the mainland.

Truffles.

Reminding people from the mainland that Princess Mary is from Tasmania.

Calling the rest of Australia 'The North Island'.

Loving Melbourne or Sydney, but definitely not both.

MONA and all of the MONA things, like Dark Mofo, MONA FOMA, Dona Mono, Dark FOMO, Fono MONO ... or whatever they're all called.

Finally having another thing to be famous for, other than being shaped like a vagina ... except that that the other thing that you're now famous for is a wall of vaginas.

Knowing someone when you go to the cafe.

Knowing someone when you go out to dinner.

Knowing someone when you go to the market.

Knowing someone at the wall of vaginas.

Being annoyed that you're stuck in peak-minute traffic.

Tickets to see your AFL team. Oh, that's right, you don't have one of those.

A pic with the Obar Bunny.

Referring to your six-bedroom holiday mansion as 'The Shack'. You've got a whole bunch of those, I see.

Finishing school at 16, then going to 'college' – which is just Year 11 and 12. So weird.

Being swooped by a magpie. Oh, no, you don't need that.

Late-night shopping. Oops, you don't need that either.

Blundstones.

A black puffer jacket, or several.

Calling that a black puffer jacket 'The Tassie tuxedo'.
Never gets old, that one.

Putting your jacket on, then taking it off when you go
inside, then putting it back on again when you go out,
then taking it off again when you go inside, then putting
it on again when there's a bit of a draft, then taking it off
again, then … I think we've got the idea there.

Wine. Lots and lots and lots of wine.

Gin. Lots and lots and lots of gin.

Thinking it's awesome that it's snowing, but then the snow
doesn't last very long and just melts away quickly so it's
just cold and wet and miserable for the rest of the week.

Being told to shut up by the other states in Jimmy's
Meanwhile in Australia videos. Sorry, it could take a while
to ring all of these up. Shut up! There's a lot of them!

Overpriced property.

Overpriced rentals.

Overpriced firewood.

Going for a hike.

Having a stand-off with a friend over whose 'neck of the
woods' you should meet in.

Bumping into Boonie down the street.

A curried scallop pie.

Stopping on the Tasman Bridge so a ship can pass underneath, through the *correct* pylons.

Being proud of negative carbon emissions.

Spotting bogans doing blockies around the CBD, because there's nothing else to do. Let's times that by ten, shall we?

A bottle of Hartz mineral water.

A six-pack of Cascade.

Or Boag's?

Or Cascade?

Or Boag's?

Or none.

The inability to drive down a road that you want to drive down in the CBD because it's one-way. Mmm ... lots of those.

When you meet someone new and are either related, owe them money or have slept with them. Even more of those, eh?

A snow jacket. Or 16.

Wearing 400 layers in the middle of winter, but still wearing shorts.

Copious amounts of vegan restaurants.

An umbrella that you take absolutely everywhere.

Checking the BOM weather map when you go through *any* door.

Taking every single visitor *up the mountain*.

Being asked if you've ever been on the *Spirit of Tasmania*, and you haven't been on the *Spirit of Tasmania*.

The ozone layer. Oh, no, you won't need that.

Getting sunburnt. Over and over, right?

A couple of champagnes on the ferry to MONA.

Tickets to a show at 'the Cas'.

A trip to the Gold Coast. And hey, if you want to know what to pack, check out the Gold Coast shopping cart. It's quite revealing. Just like them.

Having convict in your blood.

Going to see if your convict relative is on a brick.

Disassociating yourself from someone who lives north of the 'Flannelette Curtain'.

A good cricketer. In you go, Ricky Ponting. He's quite small, isn't he?

Using the phrase, 'Oh, but summer's good though.' Yeah, load up on those, for sure.

Complaining that acts and shows don't come to Tasmania, and then when they actually *do* come to Tasmania you don't book ahead because you think, 'Oh, I'll just grab a ticket at the door,' but then you forget and don't go. And *that's* why acts and shows don't come to Tasmania.

Having an unnecessary rivalry with Launceston.

A heat pump instead of an air-conditioner.

Getting annoyed at every mainlander when they ask if you have two heads. I mean, seriously. You don't have two heads, right?

Nothing open when you really want it to be. Including the entire state at one point.

Watching the winner of the Sydney to Hobart come in.

Being extremely cold but not cold enough to do the fun things like ski or snowboard.

Matching with someone on Tinder, and then quickly checking Ancestry.com.

Copious amounts of seafood.

Living in Tasmania and never seeing a Tasmanian devil.

Roadkill.

Some part of you believing that the Tasmanian tiger still exists.

Also believing that if the Tasmanian tiger *did* exist, it'd probably end up as roadkill.

And, finally, being annoyed at being left off maps. Yes, yes, we'll try to remember you next time. See you, Hobart. Next! Hi there! What's that? Who was I just talking to? Can't remember! Hahaha!

THE GUY WHO DECIDES ... CHRISTMAS

So, Christmas, sir.

Stressful. Make it really stressful, Jason! Slurrrrrrp.

Umm ... okay, sir. So ...

Chop down a tree that looks like an upside-down cone. Haha!

Why?

And put crap all over it.

Like what, sir?

Furry, gold plastic rope, Jason.

Okay.

Golden balls!

Is that it?

And silver balls!

Done?

And ugly ornaments your kids made in preschool. Ha!

When you say ugly ornaments—
>Painted clay handprints.

Right.
>And reindeer made out of bog rolls.

Sir, this just sounds like a—
>Shemozzle. Yeah.

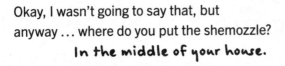

Okay, I wasn't going to say that, but anyway … where do you put the shemozzle?
>In the middle of your house.

What? Really?
>Really.

Well, I'll be putting mine out of the way somewhere, and hoping people don't see it.
>What was that, Jason?

Nothing, sir.
>Oh, and wrap it in lights, so everyone can see the shemozzle, Jason.

Sir, this all sounds a bit much. Shouldn't Christmas be a simple, peaceful time of year? It's meant to be about the birth of baby Jesus and—
>Shut up, Jason! A bearded man will fly around and give presents to people. Ha! Slurrrrrp.

Oh, okay. So he'll leave the presents at the door?
>Pffffft. No, Jason! He'll sneak into people's houses.

No! This is meant to be a nice time of year.

> Yes, Jason.

Well, people will lock the door, and call the police.

> Jason, Jason, Jason. The bearded man will watch over all the kids in the entire world.

Umm. Really? Isn't that an invasion of privacy? Won't their parents—

> And then he sneaks into their house and leaves presents ...

He doesn't take anything, does he?

> Yep.

Sigh. Really? What does he take? TVs?

> Pfffffft. No, Jason! It's a nice time of year. He takes the cookies and the milk that people leave for him.

Sir, what if someone sees him? They'll get a fright.

> No one will ever see him, Jason. Ha!

Oh, okay. So let me guess. He's lean and nimble and dressed in black.

> No, Jason! He's fat and slow, with a bright red and white suit.

Right. And no one will ever see him?

> Never.

How do people know what he looks like then?

> We'll get old, bearded blokes to dress up as him and sit in shopping centres. Hahaha. Slurrrrp.

Sigh. Couldn't we just put a picture up?

> That's a good idea, Jason.

Err, thanks, sir.

> Kids will sit on the random old, bearded man's lap, and get a picture! Good idea, Jason!

No, no. That's not what I meant.

> Ooh, and they'll get a present!

Again, this doesn't really sound—

> Shut up, Jason! Don't be a Jason, Jason.

Okay, sir. Just backtracking … you said it would be stressful?

> Because everyone has to give everyone a present.

Oh, well, that *does* sound stressful. Can we make it *not* that?

> And everyone will want whatever they've got going on in their lives done before Christmas.

Like what?

> Building, accounting, the wall painted, the garden cleaned up, the major road project completed …

The major road project completed!?

> Just kidding. That'll never get done! Ha! *Slurrrrp*. Throw another billion bucks down the toilet? Ha! What else? The contracts finalised. The grass mowed. The shed built …

Sorry, sir, but why does everything need to be done just before

Christmas? What happens after Christmas?

> Nothing happens, Jason. You just need to get it done before Christmas!

Okay, but do I even ask—

> Don't ask, Jason!

Right. Anything else?

> Yes! You have to drive all over everywhere to see every member of your family, get stuck in traffic, eat ten times the amount of food that actually fits in your body, get drunk, look excited when you open a crappy present, fill up your recycling bin three times over, burn the meat, get sunburnt, and say 'Christmas is so stressful' 400 times, before going on an overpriced holiday and getting stuck in traffic. Ha! Slurrrrrp.

Sir, I think that's too much.

> Gotta go, Jason!

Sir, no! You can't let this happen!

> Happy silly season, Jason!

What the actual flippity flips?

THE GUY WHO DECIDES ... CHRISTMAS PACKAGING

Okay, sir, we have some popular Christmas products here. Ham?

Put it in a net. And then wrrrrrap it in plastic.

Okay. And honey?

Put it a plastic-box-kind-of-bottle thing with a flat lid so it can stand on its head, with a little flap that opens to reveal a cat's anus. And when you squeeze the bottle, the sphincter opens to let the honey out! And then when you stop squeezing, the sphincter closes. Yeah-eh-eh. Do that. Slurrrrrp.

Wow. Um. Candy canes?

Wrap them in the thinnest plastic you can find, making the wrapping almost invisible. So the only way you can tell if the wrapping is on or off is by licking it.

Fruit mince pies?

> Put each one in a little aluminium tray, and then put six of them in a plastic boat. Ha! Oh, and then wrap them in plastic and put them in a box. And make the box have a window, Jason, so we can see them floating in their boat. Haha.

Okay. Plum pudding?

> Put it in clothhhh. And then tie it up with a little bow. And then put it in a plastic tub. Haha! Oooh, and then put it … in a box.

All right. Advent calendars?

> Make a cardboard box with little doors in it, with each day leading up to Christmas. Haha. And put a little chocolate behind each little door. AND THEN MIX UP ALL THE NUMBERS!

Right. And—

> I HAVEN'T FINISHED, JASON! Make sure the chocolate has got a little white tinge to it.

Okay, sir. And cream?

> Put the cream in a little plastic jar.

And we'll screw a little plastic lid on the top?

> Pffffft. No, Jason! Make half of the lid detachable from the other half with a little tab that you peel all the way around. Haha! But it doesn't go all the way around. And you use the stringy bit to pull off the lid. Yeah. Slurrrrrrrrrp.

Uh huh. And bottled beer?

> Put six bottles in some little cardboard stables. Hehe. With a cardboard handle at the top. And then

group four of those little stabley things together …
and put 'em in a box! Haha.

Okay. And so cans of beer go in little stables too?

No, Jason! Put some plastic nooses around them.
Haha. And then put four of the noosey things
together and put 'em in a box!

A plastic noose, sir? Okay. Um. Christmas lights?

Roll them up in a way that only a machine could,
and then shove them in a tub that they'll never fit
into again.

Christmas presents?

Put them in paper with Christmassy prints all over
it. And make the paper really easy to rip, even when
you're cutting with scissors. But on the odd occasion,
the scissors just sssssslide through. Haha!

Right. And Christmas presents from blokes?

Just put it in a bag! Or wrap it in newspaper and use
packaging tape.

And Christmas presents from Christmas nerds?

Wrap them in high-quality paper, with the ends
folded over perfectly, and stick it down with tape
that you can't even see. Heh. And then wrap a strip
of ribbon around one side, and maybe add a layer
of hessian, too. And a Christmassy looking bow. And
then do a special little card with a hole punched in
it—

Okay, is that—

AND because the Christmas nerd has gone to all
that effort, the person opening the present tries not

to destroy all that wrapping. But then when the Christmas nerd leaves, they just throw it in the bin. Hehe.

Olives?

Plastic tub, wrapped in plastic! With oil everywhere.

Okay. And what about a little Christmas cheer, sir?

Put a tiny packet of cards and a little joke and a little paper crown inside an old toilet roll. And then wrap it in paper and twist the ends. Haha. Oh! And put a miniature explosion in it so it goes bang when they pull it apart. Ha!

But sir—

Oh, and Jason! Make the little bangy poppy thing burn someone on Christmas Day. Haha.

Um. As you wish, sir. And what about a Pfefferkuchenhaus?

A what?

I was hoping you wouldn't make me say it again. A Pfefferkuchenhaus.

What is it!?

A traditional German gingerbread house.

Well, why didn't you just say so, Jason? Put the fragile little house on a board. And then wrap it in cellophane, so everyone knows what it is and it's no surprise whatsoever. Haha.

Okay. And what about—

That's enough, Jason! See you at the Christmas party. Slurrrrrrp.

MEANWHILE IN AUSTRALIA: KRIS KRINGLE

ACT: All right, I've sent you all a little scrunched-up piece of paper with who you've got for Kris Kringle this year.

NSW: Oh, god. Do we have to do KK? It's so lame.

QLD: Shut up, New South Wales! Just because you got a crap present last year.

TAS: Hey! Really? I thought you loved those tickets to MONA!

NSW: Urgh. I felt sorry for you, Tasmania. MONA's the only thing you've got. Whoever gets me, I need a second airport.

VIC: So you can put it on your overpriced land at Bringelly? Hahahaha!

QLD: Hahahaha!

WA: Hahahaha!

SA: Hahahaha!

NSW: Shut up, all of you! I'm checking my KK. Urgh. I've got Western Australia. Great.

WA: Well, New South Wales, I'd like you to convince the Queen to let us secede.

THE QUEEN: No.

WA: Argh, fine. Just give me a $5 billion Bunnings voucher then, New South Wales. Then I can build my wall.

SA: Let's see who I've got for KK. Ah, Queensland. Queensland, what do you want?

VIC: Get them some culture. Hehehe.

TAS: Hey! Kris Kringle is supposed to be a surprise!

QLD: Shut up, Tasmania. I'm unplugging your microphone. *Yoink.*

TAS: Hey—

QLD: And as for me, I don't need anything. Queensland is perfect. Just get me some Bundy. Or a new pair of pluggers.

NSW: It's true. You *are* perfect, Queensland. Perfectly bogan. Ahaha.

VIC: Well, looks like I've got you, New South Wales. And no, I'm not getting you an airport. How about I get you a vibe for your CBD? Because you definitely don't have one of those. Ha!

NSW: Yes, we do!

NT: You don't.

NSW: Shut up, Northern Territory! What would you know?

SA: It is kind of true, New South Wales.

NSW: Shut up, all of you! You're just jealous.

NT: Anyhoo ... I've got Victoria for Kris Kringle. So, what do you want, Victoria?

VIC: Ooh, well, hard to say. I mean, we've got the best restaurants, best coffee, culture, stadiums—

NSW: And no one can get to your city to enjoy them because you don't have a fucking airport train.

NT: I'm not getting them a train! Everyone got a train when they were three years old, all right? How about I just get you another major sporting event or something like that?

TAS: I'd like a major sporting event.

QLD: Build a bridge, Tasmania!

TAS: A bridge? I'm getting a bridge for KK?! Really?!

QLD: No! Build a bridge to get over the fact that no one cares about you.

TAS: That's mean, Queensland. I'll remember that. Well, I've got the ACT for Kris Kringle ...

WA: They need an identity! Ha.

ACT: That's rich coming from you, Western Australia. You and your 'I don't want to live here anymore'.

WA: You're right. We don't!

ACT: Well, we could do with some more land.

VIC: Yeah? Well, New South Wales has $30 million worth of land! Haha.

ACT: Ha! Good point. I'll take it for $3 million.

VIC: Haha! Good one.

NSW: Shut up! Hey, who's got South Australia in KK?

QLD: Who cares? Hahaha.

SA: *Harumph.*

QLD: Ooooh, did you see the look South Australia just gave me?

SA: Well, I'd like—

QLD: Another battery? Ha! Yeah, get South Australia another battery, and a wood-fired pizza. Hahah.

NT: So, who's got me for KK?

ACT: I do. What do you want?

NT: Well, I want to be—

NSW: A state. Yeah, yeah. You're dreaming, Northern Territory.

NT: Ha! Dreaming. Just you wait—

NEW ZEALAND: Oh, hello there, friends! Who do I have for KK this year?

ACT: Oh, shit. *Psssst*. We forgot New Zealand again.

NEW ZEALAND: You forgot me again, didn't you?

VIC: Ah, just buy something for yourself, New Zealand.

NEW ZEALAND: It just makes me a bit upset, that's all. It happens every year with you lot. I'm livid, actually. Livid!

TAS: Well, we could just do a redraw, I suppose ...

ACT: Shut up, Tasmania. Look, New Zealand, we only invite you because you're next door. It's not like this is a whole Commonwealth thing, okay?

CANADA: A Commonwealth KK, did you say? Aboot time, too.

QLD: No, Canada! You're not invited.

CANADA: Oh, dang it. I was just oot and aboot getting a two-four of Molson Canadian for everyone.

ACT: Oh, god. What do we now?

QLD: I know what to do. I hereby declare the borders shut!

WA: Yes! Hahaha!

VIC: Talk about a god complex.

NSW: That's pretty funny coming from you, Victoria. You're still going for a world record in smug mask-wearing.

VIC: Shut up, New South Wales! Your trains don't even fit in your tunnels.

NSW: Right. That's it! I'm boycotting this whole KK thing.

WA: Sounds good to me!

TAS: Guys, come on, we're all one big happy—

EVERYONE: Shut up, Tasmania!

NEW ZEALAND: *Psssst!* Tasmania, you can come over here for Christmas. But you'd better bring your sunnies and jandals. It's going to be at least 14 degrees!

TAS: Oh, wow, beach weather! I'm there!

ear Jason, wish you were here.
oking! Hahahaha. But seriously, it is
drag having to make my own drinks.
part from that, I'm in heaven and
not missing you at all. Yesterday
I yelled at the guy next door just
because he looked a little bit like you!
Isn't that funny? Yes it is, Jason.
BTW, drinks cabinet running low. Top
up please! Wait, there's someone at
the door with a delivery. That was
quick. Oh, it's a gigantic bunch of
flowers. But I'm allergic to flowers.
Who would do this to me?
Jason? JASON!?!

$3.50

To Jason

From The Guy
Who Decides

ACKNOWLEDGEMENTS

I would like to thank the left side of my brain for
dreaming up these silly characters.

And my beautiful family, especially my wife
who has no scarves or headbands left.

And Mic Looby.

And all the wonderful people at Affirm Press.

And everyone out there who has laughed at any of my content.

And coffee.

And sleep ... oh wait, don't get much of that ... thanks kids.

And did I mention coffee?